Live to the Point of Tears

by
Dan Sherven

Close To The Bone Publishing

Interior Design by Craig Douglas
Cover by Craig Douglas

First Printing, 2022

Contents

THREE | *Rivalry with The Madman*

FOUR | *High Road's Healing*

FIVE | *Image in Writing*

SIX | *Music Saves the Soul*

About the Author

Dan Sherven is a writer from Regina, Saskatchewan, Canada. He is the author of *Light and Dark*, a crime thriller. And wrote Juno-winner Classified's autobiography, *Off the Beat n' Path*. This poetry collection, *Live to the Point of Tears*, is Dan Sherven's first decade of rap. He's written more books, which will be available soon.

[Leander McLean Photography]

If you listen carefully, you can hear his daughter, Hailey, in his writing.

If this book somehow found its way to you, thank you.

Many thanks to Nick Kashuba, for ghostwriting some songs.

Live to the Point of Tears

"Men must live and create. Live to the point of tears."
— **Albert Camus**

ONE

Voices in My Head

Suicide Note

Cause' life's worth living when life's about giving
otherwise you might as well be driven by religion
flock like a pigeon to a new group decision
circumcision with precision takes away your vision
how they word it is perverted introverted Sherv heard it
not like the sheep that are asleep now here's a secret you
can keep
it's only when the building blocks fall
that you can see the composition of the Berlin Wall
I'm twisting and I'm wishing for the R.E.M. I'm missing
reminiscing on a mission to become musician and part
magician
every mathematician says it's not possible
but I've been unstoppable ever since the hospital
staring in her eyes teary-eyed I tried
but now I coincide with the growing tide of suicide
so my bride I suppose this is goodbye
cause' you don't want to try so neither do I

patient mental patient needs to repent and vent
heaven sent hell bent intent to reinvent
and it's scaring me the very thought of therapy
if you were to bury me would you see with clarity
it's a situation causing me mad frustration
I don't have the courage to express my reservation
maybe it's illumination and rumination
combining in my mind shining to make me blind
intertwined with the suppression of the expression of
depression
makes me feel less than the best I'm stressing
wishing I could escape it all

3

religion says I'm a piece of infinity's wall
divinities call but I'm too afraid to answer
laying here dismayed as I'm fearing cancer
the necromancer my life and my breath
holding the knife contemplating my own death

Inch by Inch

Stressed depressed and second best
wondering why I'm so perplexed
invest in my chest is what they said
but I can't even get the fuck out of bed
every morning there's this mourning
then there's grieving then I get breathing
achieving what I want
leaving the demon where it can't taunt
cause' the feelings reel me in the basement
but it's a big world I gotta face it
what's your why what'll make you try
what's one reason you don't wanna die
it could be simple your daughter's dimples
complex but [redacted]
leave me hurting always lurking
Spartan Sherven versing the Persians
it hurts man push on through
even if it takes some kush to do
plant yourself slant your health
climb that mountain find that fountain
and I don't blame you if you hate this
but you've gotta turn you pain into greatness
that's advice I wish I would've had
on those first nights as a single dad
I mean I was far from well
but inch by inch I crawled outta hell

with her mother I discover
she wants another lover
I'd put his name in the recording
but should Sherven mention [redacted]

5

yes pain is temporary
and so's this train ride to the cemetery
so maintain your main journey
aim to be a rap god not an attorney
I'm up early filled with fury
you're [redacted]
yeah you heard me am I not worthy
am I too nerdy the water's murky
your necklace yes I'm breathless
picket fence is on your checklist
lost in nights I can hardly sleep
Boston fights am I a creep
from the blue gin and tonic bottle
to you chronic and Aristotle
now I'm just trying to go full throttle
I won't be a bad role model
so maybe this afternoon Hails and I'll kick half a tune
with Nas in her room
represent it ain't hard to tell
the world is yours our little angel
it's a strange tale I won't compromise
in this land of living skies

These Clouds Don't Look Quite Right

I don't wanna take revenge
I'm just missing my best friend
I sit here and I pretend
that the means justify the ends
my chance to be successful
but I want romance beside the jet pool
I miss all your family gatherings
your breasts in the soap lathering
is that wrong I even miss your mom
I don't know how you moved on
it's like it didn't even hurt you
I mess every flaw and every virtue
remember when we would break curfew
December to November to smoke purple
our friends' circle fell to pieces
hope you're doing well ending your thesis
God knows you have what I want
I just have an iPod and thoughts to jot
but isn't that what I wished for
when we asked your sister to be a babysitter

when I see Hailey on the daily
she reminds me of the way you'd free me
she has all your mannerisms
I'm sorry Dan was imprisoned
one day it'll all make sense
when my lawyer makes my defense
you come to me on those nights
when nothing's right and I can't fight

sometimes I really hate you
otherwise to have loved you I'm grateful
with a plateful of chicken reminiscing
about how we talked in our kitchen
I wish I missed you because of sex
but that's not why I want to [redacted]
what's next suicidal
need a bible and a rifle at her dance recital
do you remember her first steps
what about her very first breaths
I can't lose when you're my muse
sex to Dazed and Confused or Dave Matthews

in the land of living skies
who holds your hand when you die
would you spend a life together
or does that depend on the weather
forever I've wanted you
that's the only thing that's gotta be true
am I insane be telling me
wanna hear you sing my melody
chemistry you can't deny
you can even ask Bill Nye
I can see it on your face
your past isn't something you want to erase
I don't know if I could forgive you
after all the shit I've been through
I'm just trying to tell my story
and I know you can't ignore me
you were with him drinking gin
I just wanted you to sing my hymn
I've been wondering about God
since my words make their heads nod
maybe we ain't meant to be
and maybe I should set myself free

8

a poem about you and me you turn my key to eternity
I see you with his jewelry
by the way you wear it beautifully
usually I wouldn't say this [redacted]
inappropriate shouldn'ta wrote this shit
your lawyer will probably be quoting it
when I hold our kid I remember us
all the trust that turned to rust
love and lust gone in a gust
all the seasons we had an allegiance
right up to the moment of treason
packing up your shit and leaving
then we were just friends with benefits
when I have a pen I must stencil this
genesis straight through exodus
without your love the wind's directionless

Three Little Chords

You never told me that I had a chance
woulda grown old never trying these raps
never would I ever get to spit this poetry
[redacted]
like a growing tree I'm flowing free
so careless smoking on the terrace
writing my merits before I fucking perish
should be studying German airlifts
her best buddy's probably buying her carats
three years over that relationship
three beers dread it like a Haitian chick
booze in her I'm missing her lucifer
I'd unloosen her when Grey Goose in her
a rap artist from the land of harvest
I'm the hottest and I'm the hardest
Marcus I'll carve this and take it the farthest
when I rhyme my mind's divine I shine like an asterisk
as I climb I chime in the fastest bitch
the coolest Buddhist no not Jewish like Judas
we just ran through this man I thought you knew this
influenced by Confucius and Slug's musics
don't shoot us Brutus
the lewdest rudest foolish doofus
is ripping come take a listen
dykes are like mics dripping from my spitting

a human student of rap music
the movement gets me through shit let me prove it
Chad's acoustic is therapeutic
I put elusive words to it that sound fluid
no pollutants on our tulips

you wish you could do it
be fluent be prudent
you gotta get the tools kid
we're living out our dreams lucid amusement
if you love music like Cupid be pursuant
when they say dream recruitment is stupid
be translucent there ain't no rubric
I want to improve shit and tour through Munich
write about your experience hearing this
songs come together so mysterious
serious the oblivious are delirious
who knew you too were a lyricist
using my consciousness on top of this metropolis
when I rhyme I'm in my prime like Optimus
when I rhyme more prime time than Stroumboulopoulos
you couldn't copy this if I gave you a floppy disk
consequence of these consonants is dominance
obvious I write documents from esophagus
your bitch has sloppy tits looks like hippopotamus
you gotta drop some hints you misogynist

Drugs

I used to wanna smoke marijuana
yeah I'd toke ganja with this girl Sonia
that would be my favorite flora and fauna
my persona would hot box like sauna
I loved pot like Eric loved Donna
green like iguana straight from Tijuana
she liked Madonna I liked Nirvana
but we both loved the hip hop genre
momma drove Honda after vodka
could caused trauma just like Rwanda
after lasagna pasta I wanted to give this Rasta
my anaconda but we just meditated like Dali Lama
talked about Obama going after Osama
this proper papa brought up Kafka
listened to The Beatles going through Nevada
salsa enchiladas and some soccer
she avoided drama like it was lava
talked about the stronger triple entendre
Kanye and religious dogma

ecstasy was never part of my destiny
sensibly I questioned it's recipe's chemistry
especially since an enemy deputy
would give me a nice felony penalty
so I let it be it wasn't meant for me
even though my identity has this tendency
to search for chemically produced remedies
at the embassy listening endlessly
to the legacy of John F. Kennedy
when a memory decides to remember me
I'm hit with a hellish sea of jealousy

eventually I've got to rest at peace
Sesame Street's on the television by the kitchen
he told her when it's over drink not sober
colder el Diablo than a Colorado Boulder
he stole her he holds her he sips his Folgers
she sends a text to her old flame
as he sets up sex with cocaine
Smells Like Teen Spirit Kurt Cobain
she does a snowflake proclaims her soulmate

Poets

I have a complex about deep pockets
my parents' wallets got me through college
studied politics and Big L's Ebonics
Christopher Wallace's phonics and his audience
through all this I smoked mad chronics
that much is honest I fucking promise
he's polished and flawless
thanks to the caucus of chocolates I acknowledged
I made modest deposits of profits
from speechwriting inside an office
and scholars' knowledge like Saint Thomas
August I met the hottest blondest goddess
she kept narcotics inside her closets
we used to listen to I Am The Walrus
when we lived with her parents [redacted]
vomits no omelets besides the faucets
Hailey's comet's beside the rockets
colossus good Jesus and the other prophets
this rap artist is far from novice
he's conscious that he's a garbage guitarist
they're pompous and cautious beside a park bench
where a project's lawless hard bitch frolics
boss pauses to count her losses
for some in our province there's no solace
my conscience isn't spotless
but I'm not so thoughtless to have never thought this
we buy watches that are monstrous
noxious nonsense that leaves me nauseous
on winter solstice there's few options
buying gifts at police auctions from Watson
doc says obnoxious fill their lungs with toxins
offsprings need adoptions

I use a pencil to stencil
the bass and treble of Chad's instrumentals
but what about those who live in North Central
grandparents forced into schools that were residential
how you gonna be successful with that stressful
cesspool making you feel less than special

it's like the whites are just devils
mental only focused on several lentils
how do you not burst a blood vessel
people only care about pretzels at Mosaic's temple
not a rebel I just wrestle with the existential
this is their land and they let us settle
not their parentals can't afford dental or rentals
their presidentials embezzle quit throwing pebbles
essential that we're gentle
to let ghetto petals blossom to full potential
it's dreadful whites want their entrails
or to put them in kennels like World War Orientals
so I tremble as I smoke my menthol
turn on my kettle maybe I shouldn't meddle
nah I can't take this I've got to say this
almost all of Saskatchewan is racist
what's the colour of the poorest people's faces

Green and White

Oh you have hatred for Natives
and season tickets to Mosaic
why is that combination
so popular in Rider Nation
could it be a lack of education
a sea of green hating First Nations
politicals give Aboriginals nothing
you wonder why they don't amount to something
for this track I've dumbed down the rap
so you could fit it under your Rider cap
let me guess you bought it at the stadium
no education's got your cranium hating them
have you considered the possibility
living in poverty isn't living easily
and maybe they're not all impaired
and maybe they all wanna get off welfare

I mean someone had to say it
you wouldn't listen to it from a braided Native
I've lived here my entire life
you can cut the racism with a knife
some whites say they're all alcoholics
other whites say they all rob kids

Dan you should really shut your mouth
besides you grew up in Regina south
you think sitting on your couch writing raps
is gonna help those north of the train tracks
man you should just go to Chad's

record some songs that get no response
depressing shit about your babymoms
who cares about the First Nation's sons
who care their houses have needles
they're like animals they're hardly people
it doesn't matter they have to steal copper
shouldn't you be taking care of your daughter
I'ma teach her that we're the immigrants
even a hundred bucks can make a difference
that dirty Native's gonna buy a mickey
gotta start somewhere giving change to our city
these problems don't take seconds to solve
and getting mad ain't the same thing as getting involved
I'm an Old Prince rapping to the maximum
until kingdom come in Saskatchewan

Rappers

Yeah he made it but what about the privilege
Subway sandwiches with spinach
he's connected in the business
snitch is British playing Quidditch
can't even finish his Guinness
gimmie two minutes I'll beat him in a scrimmage
he mimics Slug's image
with a fake grimace and whack gimmicks
his mistress never visits
he eats biscuits with his parents the richest
he thinks that he's the sickest
ridiculous he's not even the quickest
plus bear witness to that fact that he's fat he's got no
fitness
he thinks that he's the illest the slickest with no glitches
a monster that's vicious but he can't even sell concert
tickets
he plays with his daughter and Piglet
dirty ass hippie probably has syphilis
crew is a bunch of misfits
Ferrari Bugatti on Christmas gift list
honkey plays discus plays cribbage
and then drives over the limits
bitch ass get tested like litmus
for mental illness differences
bitterness just wanna put distances
between me and his twisted mess
don't tell me that you feel this
hell no he's not the realest
the meanest genius
[redacted]

this rap is for the rappers
the cats that rap the whack words
I could rap this backwards
and it still wouldn't be a bad verse
I could rap it faster
make the pastor say it's the rapture
I'm from the land of tractors and pastures
not Toronto's Raptors kill the laughter
after disaster you're hanging from the rafter
then this bachelor will read chapters for his Masters
you're actors your rhymes are rather whacker than this
cracker's
an attacker like a hijacker expecting someone blacker
you're slacker than a hacker that hasn't heard of Napster
tell the broadcaster I'm your kidnapper
factor in a chiropractor
from the whack rap cats who pack clappers
to the backpackers inspired by Mathers

Homecoming

I'm not really in the mood to flow
but here I am again in the studio
I'll try not to be pseudo
like that guy Trudeau yeah you know
who listens to rap in Saskatchewan
that's the question that I'm asking Dan
maybe I should quit these raps
nah I must spit 'Till I Collapse
thank you for coming out and listening
if you got joints you better be twisting them
I'm so thankful to have this chance
to be a rapper and take off my mask
for years I didn't know who I was
always escaping though sex and drugs
now it couldn't appear more clearer
I finally love the Dan in the mirror
always knew that I was a writer
you ain't seen shit can you even spell diaper
I just wanna make my parents proud
always loved me they were always around
my grandparents framed my first poem
there's so much that I owe 'em
Keegan Lloyd thought I could be a rhymer
Drake did it for Toronto I'll do it for Regina
Spencer Reid pushed me to freestyle
now rappers step to me and we smile
Matt Shepherd said I had talents
well fuck not even half of his
Graham Hilton loved my spitting
back I the basement when I was whack as shit
Chad Neald he always believed
abracadabra CD release

of course there were doubters
one of them probably had her own monsters
she was laughing when she heard my raping
boom magic mic Aladdin
the industry wouldn't give me the mic
now you gotta pay me on concert night
sent my raps to a local producer
look at me now you fucking loser
Brother Ali said be yourself
rap your heavens and your hells
now I just say what comes to mind
praying that the girls lay down quite fine
really women I'm not looking for a lover
busy swimming in album covers
I wanna tour all the way to Vancouver
and never again be in a police cruiser
I just talk about my past
and somehow cats love my raps
what's the motif of my album
separated from the X just like Malcolm
but this songs for those in the crowd
you've found the profound underground sound
I do this art form cause' you get my heart warm
what more could I even ask for
do I need a passport to be a rap star
or can Saskatchewan keep taxing him
I wanna rap all the way to Toronto
on topa that I wanna tour through Chicago

music the great communicator
these drum kits and Dan the Rhymesayer
this song is for my home town
used to write speeches about brown cows

21

and if I can get paid for this shit
just imagine what you can do kid
I don't give a fuck what your dream is
it's about hard work not being a genius
half the tracks that I write
cats think are trash they don't even like
and half the beats given to me
will never get released on our CD
so why are you still at the concert
listening to the father on the announcer
you've heard about my heaven
now go home and make your own legend
you've got to find your passion
mine just happens to be rapping
you wanna spit poetry like Sherven
easy just put the fucking work in

Where the Beats Come Free

crazy like Shady batshit
what this dad did you can't match it rap kid
this muggle doesn't know about the struggle
never had to juggle a children's puzzle
with bubbles and baths and cuddles and laughs
and snuggles and mathematics
doesn't know the magic of blankey fabrics
or rabbits he'd never had to balance his talents
with rappers that are full of malice
never had to practice not to be the whackest
so if you subtract this you better re-add bitch
never had his tactics submerged like Atlantis
prayed like a mantis Pope Francis or a Baptist
never had to bath kids like Catholics
never took his five year-old to parks Jurassic
or gymnastics ass kid never seen her backflips
he doesn't know the classic plastic Illmatic
nicotine addict raps on a tablet in a hammock
cops are only on TV and in traffic
never been a [redacted] living in tragic havoc
never gave his daughter chapstick
read Sartre and blazed with a matchstick drastic
never watched a chick flick with a fat chick
never felt fat compared to Ben Affleck
never been as high as an attic and rapped at it

[redacted] asked me out to coffee
obviously the prophecy is that she wants me
I studied philosophy she painted olive trees
she studied policy I smoked botany
it was a biography of comedy and [redacted]

23

a wobbly colony especially our economy
honesty our neurology had monotony
she modestly made this rap wannabe broccoli
she constantly brought novelty with quality
she probably unconsciously loved my biology
beautiful unusual sings like a musical
suitable to spend a life with and share a funeral
so doable I'd [redacted] like a noodle bowl
we've both worked in cubicles and had love as juveniles
now I realize I'm delusional this isn't excusable
our love's non-renewable it's reducible
to the fact I haven't found a replacement
makes me feel adjacent to the basement
she had patience like doctors or the ancients
in a Toyota Matrix taking eight hits
[redacted] are just missing her loving
which sucks cause' she's found her future husband
they're clubbing so she's out of this discussion
I hope [redacted] we're touring through London

24

TWO

Life in Death

Gone

Heaven's man's way of coping with the gone
but I don't need God if I have you in my thoughts
on Sunday June seventeenth
killed by a drunk driver we're still in grief
even though we've watched your sunset
the days and the rains face ain't done yet
how could I contemplate suicide
when I owe it to you to live two lives
how could I write this the day I heard the news
cause' you taught us it's up to you to do it huge
the brightest stars burn out the fastest
two three year olds gymnastics classes
I smoked 25 cigarettes
and learned what in life is actually significant
you had a gift for telling stories
but we won't get to hear about his Ford's keys
if you wrote a song about a who you love
would you spend that song saying a song ain't enough
poets exploit their experience
a practical success who saw through appearances
I don't know what else I could say
you taught me heaven and hell's a jump away
why was my last message to my best friend
about alcohol and stupid sex again
family's looking at your body autopsy
leaving us was the best lesson you taught me
too supportive when I'd write rhymes
bringing up the old winds of our bike rides
why were you obsessed with Christmas
rest in paradise Saint Nicholas
life love death and fate
is this escape or is this faith

your physical form's in fragments
a spiritual door though language
is this all just God's fault
two Oddballs slaying on Lockout
you taught me we're on death row
and I'm cutting in line with cigarette smoke

you had philosophical insights
but were practical and unstoppable in this life
life's too short to not be who you are
your light shines forth like a superstar
I go from rhyming and rapping
to uncontrollable crying and laughing
beautiful memories where the water falls
funeral eulogy shared by your brother's jaw
how can I sum up Nick's love
let's just say he was a real [redacted]
make your love record your album
cause' your life's journey is its outcome
I can't believe that your day's gone
I feel you playing songs by Dave Grohl
Everlong then your mom sets her love
into the afterlife as I grab your light
and try to ignite love's pain
on the road's side your blood and remains
somewhere between Amen and Satan
close your eyes and you'll see what I'm saying
man I didn't really like your nick name
so I called you by your Nick name
I miss our dumb sayings and the mundane
the same dudes after years of GameCube
it's like you've gone away on a vacation
until I die I'll probably stay waiting
it seems I'm coping with your loss
the thing is it feels like a dream Descartes

there's so much I have to tell you
a hero's journey cut short fell through
from wrestling in our basements
to biking strange kids as the rain hits
you left with what you came with
rest no anguish it never made sense
I'm holding on to what I can
the gone soul of a golden friend
is someone getting the best of you uh
rest in peace Nick Kashuba

those words written on my page
back and forth spitting with Sherv's sage
soon it'll be our birthdays
the real heroes die before they're thirty
we all forget how much life should be admired
I thought we'd die by the time of retirement
I think it's time I met with a professional
could angels be interdimensional
cause' I don't feel like I wrote this
someone's watching over both my shoulders
cracking jokes with the hardened demon
and snatching flows from the Garden of Eden
even though you never believed Gospel
your picture and obituary are a novel
people I've never even heard about
are spreading your good news through word of mouth
in the cemetery you're above ground
only makes sense since you're in the clouds
how am I supposed to summarize
the sun of life when the son won't rise
you gotta dance to life's loud song
cause' it lasts but you don't know how long
now wow my goodness gracious
all I know is that your footprints saved us

I never took you to Cheeky's performance
but I bet now your seats are gorgeous
I wrote this mostly for us
if only I could sing this chorus
you're lost forever in that forest
the frosty weather is the boldest
the thoughts that matter the most important
past present and future in a recording
I wanted you to hear me on that podcast
but clearly you're busy listening to God's raps
you pushed me not to smoke but exercise
it should be me who rests his eyes
right after the day that you died
I started making music about your life

I remember we crashed on the parkway
in December you gave cash to God's flame
not only did you support a poet
but with no lord you afforded the homeless
my attempt will never suffice
but what's left but to try to write
what am I supposed to say to my dead friend
who left and then bled bled bled
sent into the air on the highway
two best friends spoke on Friday
work ethics views and IQ
they find you dead on arrival
from the Foo Fighters to Led Zeppelin
killed on the highway as a pedestrian
we've met again and left the wind
I'd say your end let's me begin
your ex-girl said put it in words
Nick I'll never have enough of your hurt
I can feel you in all the music
laughing to myself looking clueless

you were a man that had life's blueprints
my pen won't tie up those loose ends
maybe now you're with the God
saying that this song is way too long
but it's the least that I can do
trying to bleed though you and your truth
writing this was just a controlled accident
like your tragedy beyond imagining
but I'll see you up in the next life
better fucking save God's best mic

The Truth

Shining in the darkness redefining hardship
what you even know about belief in God's gift
too intelligent I rap for the hell of it
skill well hell for real you better develop that
push the envelope shush 'em with sounds so dope
it's impossible you don't cross your toes
I lost my soul at the cross roads
and found hope and more in what Nas spoke
gone in smoke is my voice
that's a worst fear since that first year
but now my night terrors are quite rarer
maybe cause' I fight fair or always write prayers
regardless the darkness is dog shit
use your light beams to keep shining
when they ask me how do you define Dan
catch him replying my man I am

nothing's impossible if you lock on your goals
act responsible and not talk to ghosts
of course smart has a good horse
but hard work and heart always took first
I guess I didn't need to record this
you heard the stories bout the hare and the tortoise
man I just thought it was important you have a purpose
like Sherv has as the wordsmith perfect
sometimes you'll feel worthless
but no you don't deserve death
take that from a schizophrenic
whose disease made Cheeky beyond God and hellish
and hell still I live
yo will they forgive Dan for his sickness

I doubt it
give him a guilt trip but I ain't drowning
in life's great fountain
now feel that realness

motherfucker I'm The Logos
oh you don't know those words it's something God
wrote
into Being it's the sinful demons
miserable feelings got you sniffing coke in the evenings
even when believing it
got nothing to do with Jesus
now you're seeing Dan be a friend
not a biblical imbecile
I'ma flip this shit like reciprocal integrals
man I'm in the flow
trying to live life priceless
like Christ did
or the Buddha man the truth is raw
nah the truth is ruthless I don't gotta prove shit
cause' the music is
and my promises are obvious
and yo my esophagus is the start of his
wisdom rhythm
and what's given
plus a future always unwritten
running down the hallways within man

Psycho Logical

Maybe he felt guilt when he killed Nick
maybe he didn't I don't know his spirit
but what's clearer to this weirdo
is after the collision that asphalt killed them both
imagine causing the accident
they handcuff him passenger in the backseat row
the police cruiser going on tour whew
yeah he had a booze a few what that's news to you
the problem is they couldn't solve it quickly
because of Nick's drinks
I don't know nor will I tell you everything
but he was out celebrating some friends' wedding rings
a tall gown in a small town getting locked down
Nick went to walk around but got locked out
no keys phone or jacket
so he hit the streets all alone with no wallet
to grab a cab with
walking on asphalt

asphalt but no malice or guilt trip
it's just tragic that Nick's dead
forgiveness for the killer's liquored liver
so I'm not as bitter as our city's frigid blizzard
since you've killed our friend but you can live more
Dan I'm gonna get in trouble for not shoving
smacking you with a shovel or shouting fuck you
but dude one human life's gone
I don't really see the point of duplicating the sum
plus what would it accomplish
sending your mind and body to rot in jail's dark pit
obvious

34

not to mention since alcohol and its thoughtlessness
was the cause of death
Nick was drunk walking on the asphalt
cops got called cause' he was almost hit
before you arrived drunk and driving
Saskatchewanian

will Nick's ash fault me for talking so honest
I doubt it he knows that's all I got left
I could never write rhymes so spiritual
without the guidance of My Hero's soul
I'm a conduit for God truth and Nick
if that wasn't obvious your full of nonsense and bullshit
I don't need a pulpit I leave emcee's skulls cracked
with bullets from my soul and lips
that'll put a hole in the hull of your ship
and keep you null and void I think I stole part from
Keegan Lloyd
back before Cheeky has his own voice
now I destroy all noise
keep it quiet speak in silence
grieve Nick's iris see him in my eyelids
blinded shining accidental violence
grabbed the soul of my friend
I ask the Lord why again
did this happen to Nick

Game Over

Here we go you're terrible now rock this on your stereo
I'ma beat your ass so bad that your arrogance folds
it'll be your burial I'm over your head like Mario
I'm underwater helicopter either way I'm Ariel
we ain't comparable I hit you with a parable
I be the prodigal son but I'm a methodical one
a philosophical bum unstoppable on drums
using my biological logical module every molecule
to rock a fool and drop a jewel it's hip hop I rule
that's obvious I hit you with these documents
no it don't matter what the rapper's topic is
the audience gets lost in it I'm talking about my
consciousness
it's infinite like Nicholas I'm so slick with this gift
that it's ridiculous like the level at which Nick was
meticulous
rest in peace to my great friend
this beast on beats don't need to raise the dead

I grabbed the keys to happiness
they're called rapping on these beats that sound like
Minneapolis
yo you think the galaxy is a catastrophe well nah b
I think you mean a masterpiece that is Cheek
put my piece on the parchment
this artist was standing outside up in the darkness
when all of a sudden love winned and sparked us
cars and gents carcinogens ashes fly
told her I'm the arsonist well a narcissist who raps fire
her mouth finds words
either way believe when I say I'm off the meter bae

even Saint Peter gotta pull the lever someday
once they love hate and make the devil wait
and chase after heaven's gate
ladies and gentlemen
then your adrenaline is destined to win listen
to this veteran of rhetoric
and let it live

nah fuck rhetoric I'm a genetic freak of poetic speech
and all a this was meant to be
I came through the centuries like a centipede
like a penitentiary like an advent wreathe
what's the message from this schizophrenic
pick the pen up young pup and be a legend
choose beats that make you feel aggressive
loose leaf and true speech is the zenith
and when it's time to end my life sentence
know I was the master but mostly an apprentice
your favorite rapper must have a death wish
that little effort and putting Dan on the guest list check it
my style's reckless like this thoughtless
car crash that left Nick gone in ashes
but alive in songs and raps the time we have is
precious
friendship

If and When

Yo you was building buildings
and I was a Christian scribe under living skies
women's eyes we'd often talk about
but it's hard when you got God on your mouth so shout
you ran the villages I was a man on a pilgrimage
I can't even really tell you what the difference was
Nicholas
life ain't a life till you live it right
gimmie the mic and lemme tell you bout this Christian
scribe
all day studying the bible
you was busy in the city fucking up rivals
for sure we worked with way different titles
but came from the same life force you and I know
no Nicholas I don't mean religious shit
I mean the way of living we had the same opinions
if and when we meet again I'll see you then
I don't believe in the end because I grieve your death
I'ma set it off like the death of god like Nietzsche
you needta to some research and reading
I'm the rap fiend caffeine and nicotine
to split your spleen and live my dream

maybe I'm delusional for keeping your human skull on
my desk
when you're gone in death I met dawn at dusk
and forgot what love really meant
till I watched the city's little pretty tears swept away for
decades
forget the migraine headaches
and everything that death brings checkmate

we used to play some chess underneath the summer's
heat
if only we could make it last but we didn't and you
killed him
now I'm feeling like God was the villain for real man if
and when
I find forgiveness hope I can live it
and Nick's death gives strength maybe it was meant to
be
it's crazy a great deed heaven sent for thee
lately I break free shape these advent wreathes
painting scenes of my strange dreams to make peace
Nick is king in my castle asshole and so I have gold in
the rap flow chateau
the plateau I smash through go ask the fool
court's jester bout The Lord's professor

I lost a great merchant a friend of Sherven
and still for real I been spilling cursive
tryna to worship in these churches
at night Daniel's candle writes verses heard this
yo you were killed by a horse carriage
Rough Riders the driver was drunk and careless
big surprise his her eyes saw it all
God and his faults not at the cross walk
the lost cause taught us many things
not to be envious cause' death'll bring
jester and his king to our doorstep
before there's more war to endure left
this existence who am I kidding
maybe you didn't and you still walk among the living
if and when Nick is dead give us our daily bread
to make peace for our friend rest in paradise
I'm blessed to have shared your life
but the arrogance of this scribe

won't carry the way you thrived
now you're buried alive inside the living skies

Say It Now

Couldn't let them do that to me
cause' you know the truest emcees
bleed through the papyrus I don't care who your label is
try to step to this exorcist my beats make necks just twist
turn your favorite emcee into a pessimist till the death of
us etcetera
understand this I'm breaking through the canvas
Dan is madness sadness and blackness
take it apart break it into art
use that baggage to my advantage climb rhyme status
ladders the fastest you can't touch that
the track you feel isn't Chad Neald
I'm the producer overseen by Nick Kashuba
he's overseas booking tours for the rapper slash
entrepreneur
who's coming to New York
I ain't a big shot I don't want a wrist watch
I just wanna hip hop until I'm with Nick and God

I got a fat belly but what else could you tell me
I ate too much of your girl's KY Jelly [redacted]
they told me to go to open mics
while they spend they whole life just smoking pipes
I know the dice cause' I rolled a paradise
became a parasite to tear the mic where I like
share my light through vocal expression in the solar
system
locals listen even if they don't know what's within Dan
wow sir no you're a Bowser
words nah nonsense
God gifts the fire flower

41

redefining what's alive in Regina ours
the Queen City I dream like Biggie
you've seen me Cheeky freestyling
speech and light bends so does writing
the pain of her last name being hyphened
I'm a bright man with a life plan
aight then

yo your judgment fuck it you can't touch this
yo snorting the substance straight from the justice
break it apart man it's just us trust that
yo the government broke the covenant and got no
punishment
your favorite creative don't want none of it
I send 'em to Euphrates Hades or Nunavut
what is this miraculous rapping gifts
don't ask for Dan I pass on a feature
like it was cannabis man I plan to win
I'm going into the dark side like Anakin
and again I'm ravenous with this spectacular shit
vernacular splits where the tarantulas spin
the spider's Webb and in this rhymer's head
I see Regina's mess when the curtain falls
Sherven's soul is a writer's death

Keep It Real

I don't know if it's real but her feelings
are gonna get hurt so I'm loving in the verse
us competition the love's within Dan
but at the same time I'm gone with the wind when
I start to realize her heart and her eyes
aren't what I want cause' I been on this path
for way too long walking until dawn always alone
unless of course you count God
beyond this to be honest I don't know if that's what I
really wanted
I thought if this hot mess of pot breath and bought
cigarettes
could give me some [redacted]
I'd see her as a goddess but it turns out we're just not
friends
so what am I really chasing shit definitely not one
relationship
just [redacted] it leaves me with facelessness and my
ancient gift
for patience slips as the patient is needing medicine
the estrogen so let him in I'll give adrenaline knowing
my pen will win
just don't expect of him to become your best friend
unless your genesis begins and ends with a kiss
that just wants to dance in the rain

I don't know if it is but I'ma flow my gift
never holding it in even if osmosis lives
and tries to grab me man I have been
one of the dopest at rapping in a way Lennon can't
Imagine

43

have her spazzing having an [redacted] she can't even
fathom
and that has been in the past tense
watch the way I grab this and bring it to the present
remain a legend as the pain of the reverend that God
locked out of heaven
was feeling that at the Seven Eleven he saw Jesus' war
inside the convenience store and never knew about the
meanest lore
that burst forward and hurt your Lord so yo I curse more
I'm unbelievable believe the flows I'm so unbelievable
I'm bleeding slow
across dimensions a boss without a best friend so I'm
stressing
for the moments but this poet be the dopest
ya'll is hopeless I been this focused since before 06
nah I stole that straight from the great Old Prince
oh if your nose drips from coke sniffs you're not sick
I'm a smart emcee your whole love is bogus
I foretold this prophecy

Can't Explain It

Man with that record I was thinking that I could be
fresher
shoulda worn a dress shirt next semester I be your
professor yes sir
often lost when walking frost bit talk then to Brahmin
and a forgotten god lives why's that an option
I don't need your notes fam I just make my points when
I be showing wisdom that's the way I goes in
ya'll don't even know Dan I told them I'm no man
I'm a poem nah an ocean frozen and the hole I'm in
is closing oh then the oxytocin rocks me close as
the ghost's sin spoke again in my veins
and heart piece this artiste carved this bark speeches
like dogs do cause' God's view was all inside of me
until I divide and flee and finally die at peace
rewind my beats vinyl releases and IQ bleeding
weakness and the deepest secrets Jesus feel it

I let go of the devil's echoes set in stone
saw the death of rose in the bed of snow and smashed
the pedestal
and when it hits the ground I grin and smile
it's been awhile since this was now
in the present moment the effort of emotions
was technique pouring and hope lived mostly
the stories were bold when the door key opened
more of Dan and his diaphragm why is The Lamb alive
again
robbing revenge of all of his strength
I don't know what common sense thinks
documents stain

people party life away
living sleepless
hardly a surprise then they don't know what dreams is
but who am I to judge
music's alive
do or die
don't let the truth lie

vividly images bleed a sick emcee kicking these
epiphanies
and pictures you see in soliloquies infinite degrees of
symphonies
the minutes scream Nick is here he never disappeared
this shit's for real let me get you a beer or two
a hero and a weirdo egos who bleed truth
an artist with cigarettes and an architect with God let's
not forget
when my lawless charge was trapping Dan inside the
darkness
of Saskatchewan's living skies you were offering
your profits to be spent to stop the long arm's grasp why
a question for my dead friend
good thing your footsteps cure death
but we're left wondering if you lived to be a hundred
and ten
what would have been

Mind of Darkness

I have paranoid schizophrenia
and it tears a void in all of the friends of ya
anxious baggage I carry that
is it arrogance or his heritage
temperament tell his therapist
hairy fists cherry [redacted]
they shared a kiss I bear this guilt
which burns me you heard Cheek
prefers beats where Sherv thinks deep
I'm allowed now by the ten thousand hours
pens vowels nouns words
to massacre the passengers
around the globe now you found Sherv
word then prefer it conservative
I disturb the kids with endurance performances
you've never heard before thus
my purpose is cursive that is honest and flawless
but I know that you never thought different

philosophically Socrates who talks on beats
lost in the deep end no cheating on the weekend
please don't feel Dan
even Eden's Eve n Adam had 'em demons
get rid a that allegiance and you're free again if
I'm Anthony Kiedis type a genius
I'm Royal 2 destroying you and peeling wigs
rise from the cigarette ashes phoenix
in my life time I write rhymes
let my light shine from my bright mind
so why am I alive maybe it's just not quite right
that I die fine

I'll just focus on the quotients that wrote this
while he'll demonstrate his pen is great
a lyrical renegade living in the devil's face
trying to be generous
give the benefit of the doubt
despite my independent thoughts
of what's not

I been the accuser I been the loser
I been the boozer I been the loose-end
I been the lucifer I been the medusa
these are true words I been living human
where's Kashuba I need to talk with Nick
my consciousness just caught its grip
as I was walking up in the forest
where the monsters live and it was so horrid
horrible deplorable my war will grow
my oracles knows unless I grow my soul
and realize the real lies weren't
in my real eyes but what analyzes
Dan's demise is my mind's abyss
imagination imagine hatred imagine sacred
imagine naked imagine faceless
even if it don't make sense

Put Your Soul In

Eyedea had a line I was built to climb
that really makes me feel fine that makes me align
I been working on this record for a minute
still I feel like nothing I do is ever good enough for
Nick's love
think I never struggled wasn't hungry yeah I got it
honkey
my story is everything you wouldn't stupid
a writer documents his internal journey
using causes from the external world for real
it's dopaminergic so I spoke these words to Nick
I need dope I mean I need dopamine
psychosis diagnosis but hope lives
since his prognosis is no symptoms
medicine is stopping hallucinations
you ever seen God's causes improving your faith fam
I was driving my car and saw a giant guardian
a demonic rabbit a sonnet of my madness

rap is the evolution of jazz blues and rhythm
avenues infinite affluent infants
are you listening Dan's news I give it to 'em
I rapped the fruit of Nick's spirit but he built this
pyramid's roots
I just added the periods shoot I missed one
this album is a time capsule binded with thoughts and
more
that've got to hurt
this is Nas meet Sherv nah it's really Costanza meets
George
Seinfeld I rhyme well Einstein will cosign how

my energy compares to an mc squared
prayers in the air won't spare your tired ass
a tire wrench won't wrench my attire facts
I'm a distinguished English linguist
Vintage like the Vinyl my IQ you couldn't climb and
view
die fool my rhyme pool be the deepest
but I hit the drive thru like I'm in high school eating

think in the clouds and work in the dirt
Sherv's eternal verbals burn holes like inferno
in my personal journals
emcees be pissed off like urinals
I Blastoise [redacted] like Squirtle
words flow like Virgil's cursive notes
through Sherven's throat these are murderous quotes
don't hold that rope so close you'll choke I know
the day the musician dies you play him and you listen
fine
this is Plato meets Aristotle
I bomb emcees like NATO with collateral damage
I woulda said hospital but that's too savage
this dad is of the baddest status
your average asses can't match this
I couldn't open for Classified's local show
a year later I'm chosen to wrote his book
how's that for persistence
bowing to Nicholas
the mind the intellect

THREE

Rivalry with The Madman

Y

Why did you die and I'm alive
am I supposed to write your life
while you fly through the sky
making it right for my time
I don't know but I'm gonna rhyme
you said to tell the story
but in my head hell has no glory
yet there's redemptive qualities
when I pick the pen up and give all of me
writing is my therapy
life gets better when you do you ask Gary Vee
I barely breathe these days
waiting for emails about Cheeky's pages
sacred ancient creations
that might save Dan from being basic
and ways of living like hatred
and becoming an aimless vagrant
that's why

Y is a letter with a long long tale
and I write letters and songs with Hails
that's my daughter and I ain't got words
for how strong she makes her dad's verse
I had her at nineteen
and without her I'd be a piece of shiet
sorry I gotta be honest
there's just more to me with my daughter
now how're you gonna be a factor
wow this is way bigger to me than rapping
that's why there's no competition
it's just me and my own inner vision

plus my old friend Nick and
my only children's soul within Dan
so while I'm still living
I go to the well in the building that built the man

Can't Hit Me (Improvised)

Knights of the sound table I write the bound fables
that create you and shape you like Plato
I might break through go and play some GameCube
pick some wigs on The Pit in Halo
I'm the same dude that I always was
except I run down the hallways with the rugs
and the hallway it changes like a maze does
and then I wonder what leaves us in amazement
it's hard to tell but God will prevail
if you didn't know I scribble flow plus I got a schizo
dome
so why you think I'm a divine speaker
probably cause' you can feel my mind reach yours
I'm intelligent and you is irrelevant
I'ma squash a fool talk jewels like an elephant wait
you never heard the elephant speak
well you know for real you is irrelevant and fake

I grab 'em by the throat when the divine spoke
I'm just a channel who goes by the name of Daniel
and so I'm an asshole have some tadpoles
if I rap the ghost then I might attack yours
yes I exist in-between dimensions
sound and space I'm allowed the face you can't get in
cause' I be such a different dude
with a cigarette mood you an insignificant view true
and I do this for Nicholas
I push the boulders up my shoulders like I was Icarus
wait
Sisyphus I'm burning my wings
either way I know you heard him and it rings

in your earrings
lyrics that are spirits
what you even saw well it was in his
own dome before it came out of my throat
and then I spoke and you know that I'm the goat

the beats and the lyrics
they speak and you hear it
so you can understand this canvas is near Dan
if you didn't then you was probably kidding your whole
life
man I sit with a gold mic
on a gold throne it's time for me to go home
so I decided to freestyle an album
I'm a beast child I'm a beast when I'm rhyming
[redacted]
but it's more like autograph signing
shining like a diamond that's how I been
why you even trying I'm alive then
you're a dying man
cause' when I step to the mic devices
knowing that my life is priceless
it suffices that I be the dopest
and you is just hopeless
you don't have the focus of the poets no sir
might fuck around and write a novel
just to drop some knowledge the college won't allow
though

I Need To

I need to fucking practice
filthy habits cigarette packages and of course Nicholas'
ashes
that is my surroundings you found Dan under the
mountain
yeah you know the one
where you're exhausted
everyone talking is too much the cost of a friend
you wanna rush to bed feel the rush of lust and so that
text you send
yet exorcising demons are calling you
you should walk and talk to God under Autumn moon
true
but the fall's in view and the blues they sound like jazz
only rap's allowed
now what am I to do
well first on my list is the curse and the gift
Sherv must worship at churches of verses
a writer
otherwise my life is a nightmare

I need to fucking practice
I ain't dying living average
that does not mean status got it
cause' shit Dan is talented
with the valiance of a champion
yeah I'll battle your man
I'll slap a rapper straight outta Saskatchewan
wait fam this is getting whack a bit
I was exhausted but now I'm toxic
I talk shit but got no message

57

irrelevant aggressive penmanship yet again
coffee got me talking
but I need God's speech on Broad Street
with what K-OS thinks
inspiration in spirit amazing
but lacking the mind's oasis
basin's gone dry
and so I must try to touch the most high
and flow the mind's creations
before I'm gone in the graveyard
dead again

I need to fucking practice
I can't stand this
all these rappers thinking they'll make it happen
but that's just distraction
how come my song about writer's block
is better than your deepest thoughts
oh wait this game is like golf
so you don't need to worry bout my big bad wolf
I almost defeated him
but evenings give him strength
when I'm tired he's inspired
when I'm wired he's on fire
I burned that bitch
threw him in the furnace
and got that door locked
but his forms are plentiful
so the devil works
when your pencil's broke
this message is old for a reason
demons creep in on the weekend
while you're sleeping
what do you need then
a meaningful purpose

to kill the devil's soul merciless
I can hear him again

Beautiful Dreamer
(Improvised)

My stomach hurts and I'm done with Sherv
I plummet to the Earth but I run through a verse
something to do loving for you
but it's troubling when I'm Bumbling without a view
who knew the VooDoo like Hendrix
I'm a mix between him and Kendrick
but I didn't die at 27
maybe a legend when I get to heaven
but it seems unlikely unless it's just the writing
of books love the hooks
but this chorus starts to bore us when there's not more of
us
I saw Ouroboros in the forest just
beside the sorceress and I had contorting thoughts
they was grabbing me then I rapped and freed
the pieces of my mental a beast without a devil
as I let go and offer forgiveness
and then become a rapper with Nicholas

it seemed impossible it seemed I lost my soul
but then the audio it taught me some new Notes
from the Underground with the summer sound
and the winter blizzard it starts to kill my words
and I feel the urge to just sit on the mattress
maybe BioShock Atlas
I'm alive and my thoughts are Rap Shit
so who will buy this I don't know but it's violence
in my mind's eyelids and in my iris
I see Sirius but I just keep on shining

why am I alive then
to be a dope dude the one who spoke truth
no one can control who
has they own mind this is like a goldmine
in Mozambique man my flows damn deep
you know the man Cheeks
he's the poet and the writer
alright I'm going too hyper

I'm far from perfect like the stars above Earth is
up inside the heavens my mind is a weapon
and I'm using it just as the muse will sing
inside of me until I die at peace
you can find the Cheeks not in the cemetery
but the one who is blessed with vocabulary
spectacular when it comes to the vernacular
I asked Hailey to kill Skyrim's tarantulas
they be grabbing ya I need a bigger spatula
that has a double shield you is just a muggle for real
and I don't give a shit about Harry Potter
if you read that you're barely an author
I'm rarely a rap star I don't want a Jaguar
a fast car I'll freestyle in a Rav 4
and ask for a passport
so I can get outta Canada
and prove I'm more than a rapper amateur

Tell the Story

I was just a kid with a philosophy degree
thinking I should slit my wrists and let it all bleed
a teenager who was a parent
a dream chaser now that's apparent
I was almost jailed almost lost Hails
spent some days in mental health inpatient unit true shit
who is this is it Cheeky
not anymore God answers prayers
even when you never ever thought that he was up there
wait what am I trying to say
be honest work hard with purpose and endurance
you can persevere this near-death experience
divinity's spilled his ink on this lyricist
with periods and epochs of deep thought
to believe in God

but hey I'm just a born sinner
so I mistake a storm for a winter blizzard
still though
I learned how to tell the truth
in doing so the muse's tunes burned hell's roots
well for the most part
no not really a Mozart
I'm more of a lost in thought
who jots his heart in the dark until
then the story screams by its own vocal chords
I still can't believe I got to meet Luke Boyd
they flew me to Enfield because they knew my pen is
real
so Dan and a hero taking a steering wheel
down to the weed store

guess journalism school was worth the thousand zeros
he rapped Half Life and I get to write his story
Classified

it's weird though cause' he's a hero
but I want to be lyrical so where do I go
his auto-bio is nearly done
but my lyrics remain unsung
and my introversion it begs the question
do I really need the stage's blessings
but when I hear these lyrics
epiphanies scream at me
it's just like I love the art form
but I don't know if I want a life of talking
talent for rapping I've got some
but I'm content in my hot room writing
when my life ends will I regret it
if I never grabbed the mic with the lord's blessing
well isn't that the question
hey Class man
you wanna check this song

That Breeze (Improvised)

Non-stability with the monster will in me
that kills responsibility you feeling like all of Cheek
on the olive tree that's where I stand under
rap blunders don't matter cause' the map's getting
smothered
by the dome piece of Cheeks
that's the way that I love these trusting beats
that hit me and drop these epiphanies
killing these little millipedes that was never real to
Cheek
dropping butterflies don't need her mother's thighs
or some brother's crimes
that intertwine in my simple mind
then the Tinder guy emerges
this is where Sherv lives inside the wordsmith
he's in my chest dying 'til my death
I'm alive with my final breath
and the cigarettes they are rummaging
inside my pockets unlocking the struggle within

that breeze it raps within Cheek
when I go for a drive in the Accord yes my mind does
explode
listening to K-OS' great thoughts
trying to praise God under some rain drops
that's Atlantis you don't know the Rap Shit
you ain't practiced for a decade
lived with the headaches
still get the check and paid for an auto-bio
God flow my mind though
understand me I'm breaking through the boundaries

I found peace and it was a thousand leaves
and they allowed my speech to go to a higher plane
I'm redefining Regina's flame
because they all the same
they don't bring that divinity
so when I spit and free the pieces that will live with me
then I'm going to a higher plateau
yes you understand the writer's rap flow and so

I don't have much to say
I just love the day
and I pick up the pieces by using telekinesis
when I was 12 I went to hell for snubbing Jesus
but that's a Nas rhyme guess we both share God's mind
that be God's plan this is like a hot flame
that might be burning Lord have mercy
I curve these little pieces of the puzzle
I'm a beast with no muzzle
I release then I guzzle
it's the thesis the struggle
what more
I'm the dopest ever so I'ma choke this treasure
and I hold it to heaven
it gets even higher
when I'm the one to redefine all the fire
that be burning me and now you heard a Cheek
well I deserve to be worldly like Turkey on the stage
you heard me it's deserving of the praise
which you do have
welcome to the true raps

Your Door

now she's pregnant somehow I'm schizophrenic
but I'm glad we ended cause' I don't want a wedding
our adventure of our placenta ties us together
till dentures are up on our agendas
I remember the winter's info sessions
living at your uncle's as I rush to my lectures
somehow I got a 92
maybe it was my dumb smile writing views on life and
truth
I don't wanna argue with you
our issues have passed
everything we've been through shattered like glass
when the vase breaks and makes shapes
down on the floor you can try recreating what you had
before
but you're liable to cut yourself
I would know I've done that
metaphorical never a mortal wound
I wrote this poem for you
cause' I ain't showing up at your door anytime soon

you can love without being in love
and maybe that's what I'm trying to get across
once I was talking with Andrew
and he said one of those thoughts that always nags at
you
said the worst part of his parents' divorce
was that they couldn't even share the same house
I don't mean live together just sit with each other
and I've thought about it over the months and years
I've grown colder with age that's for sure

but I just think it's better for her if I don't let it burn
maybe I'm immature and should grow up
learn it's okay for me to show love
but it just hurts way way too much
so don't expect me to show up
your door shut my toe stubbed I'm over it

the new son's rising or is it a daughter
either way your husband's no longer just a stepfather
I feel like I should feel bothered
but if I'm being honest I'm not since
I heard the news it's good for you
true even I thought I would be jealous
cause' I'm always selfish
I gotta tell it how it is
it'll be weird when our kid is a stepsister
but she's quite fierce she'll be fine I'm sure
and as for Sherv
I've got a new perspective
the things we search for in life are too different
corrective vision arrives in 2020
you want a family
and I've got fantasies of Danny onstage
and handing in a manuscript
that makes my dead friend live Nick
so I'm no longer broken
but these days don't expect me on your doorstep
I'm over it and I just don't think

You Can Have It
(Improvised)

Should I be embarrassed that I live with my parents
well you can hear my arrogance because it barely fits
I share this gift and my style is permanent
disturb the kids conservative you have never heard of
him
well welcome my style is seldom heard on the radio
even though I got like the greatest flow
like the gravy yo up on potatoes
I gotta make Hailey a bagel but no tomatoes or mayo
they go to a different understanding
I'm slamming
all a those that fall with they flows
they could not even get close to the shit that I've spoke
whoa how are you so high on yourself
maybe because I never even lie with my breath
now it's time for me to go outside
got a cigarette put the mouth to my fire
oh man that is just going like a poem
who even knows him there's no foretolding
of this because I love the gift
which I express
this is my death

nah you can't handle it Daniel is miraculous
only thing I'm scared of is tarantulas
they be crapping me in the backseat
when I'm freestyling in the taxi
that's Cheek actually police cruiser
what you know about the beast Nick Kashuba

obviously nothing you gotta be fronting
you could never grab the mic in this month fam
cause' my month extends through the years though
and with this my pen is in your earholes
but you know that I never really puncture
I just rupture your cupboard
and fuck up your whole structure
what more
I have this cleverness
and you know that you could never handle it
cause' my style goes off the handle when
I'm freestyling and I'm a man again
that is when
I came from the spirit realm
what you even saw well you was fearing him
as you should cause' I'm a dope lyricist
periods and ink
pyramids have been built

Better Late Than Never (Improvised)

The rest will follow cigarettes at the condo
and then I get in my Accord and rock slow
I got some Nas yo and it's hitting me
Illmatic as I live and free and kill rap shit
I be driving down the streets down
doing what I can to feel these deep sounds
pretty soon I arrive at The Exchange
ready to rhyme my brain but I gotta get paid
actually it's just journalism school
so I'm there for not like a few thousand zeros
but still though I look through the window
of the brick wall and then live in full
pop a pimple and then I go inside
to flow my mind and try to know the divine
I was only there to take some pictures
but at the battle rap tournament I had to kick words

Youneak he was true with the beat
he was like on the stages I just wanted to be famous
not in the sense of making the world spin
but just the people in the building knowing Sherven
you had some girlfriends that was with you
and I was grabbing the mic hopefully with some issues
after I went and took a few pictures
I had to put my name down just to kick words
so I scribbled yours into that final
it was you versus I the battle of the IQ
in the tournament the earnings weren't big
with the championship this Campion kid

needed an Ambien shit
I'm sleeping on you I'm breathing these tunes
I'm needing a view that's higher
maybe God could find words
for me to express
cause' you is gone up above

you and I we both have the writer's curse
doing whatever we can to put our life in verse
and we had way different styles
but I can tell that playing it makes us smile
cause' you said my tracks got you in your feelings
and your whole crew too
I felt that in my Cheek man
that's like my alter ego
but now you is gone on the altar I need to flow
and I don't even really fucking know you
but it's just the fact that I gotta go through
something when another emcee who is rapping dies too
then the final
analysis you climbed the garden walls the fastest just
to drink the Holy Chalice first
yo homie I know you had the baddest verse
called me Bob Proctor and Mr. Rogers
aw damn

FOUR

High Road's Healing

Angels and Demons

I got angels and I got demons
Nick's trying to save you from being a freak again
speaking to Dan through the audio
avoid the devil at the cross roads lost soul
told me once my focus on lust
was because I hadn't done enough dope stuff
I wasn't satisfied with the day or the night
and that is why snapchat lights my life
and if you ask Jordan Peterson
he'd say I should be recording cause' it's meaningful
no not Cheeky's balls
but the deepest thoughts I can scrawl
and if God's involved it's obvious
it's my fault
these documents though pull me straight from hell
and at the end of the day
the only man I can blame is myself
and I'm feeling well

I got angels and I got demons
Nick's trying to save you from overthinking
ex-girlfriend worrying
or other people's opinions straight burying Dan
it's not important keep recording
a freeman like Morgan Gordon Half Life Classified
as long as I'm satisfied with how I rap and write
I can pass from this life
and when you looking at my epitaph
make sure you put on that shit that he was blessed with
rap
etcetera whatever you wanna put

cause' I'll be gone up in the stars Dali Lama's hood
and when I arrive at Heaven's Gates
I hope I get to rhyme right in the devil's face
lucifer was a student of music
but he never had a producer like Nick Kashuba

I got angels and I got demons
Nick's trying to make you see what you believe in
you forgave them it wasn't as bad as you thought
they was telling the truth and I'm not
out for revenge or out for they death I'm out for my
strength
I've suffered long enough
I don't think I need another thought
about just what happened damn it
I can't stand this
always thinking rewinding back words
seven years of the devil's curse
but it's what makes me so eloquent in verse
yes the obsession of Sherv ends now
fiction is way less strange than our own world
and I had to get this off my chest
cause' Dan ain't living in the past
that's death

Higher

One life divided by sun and knight
and I must write just to touch the light
once I've made a name
will I still want to play the game
that created my brain
I ain't in it to become famous
the minutes ticking away as the day shifts
remember your death is inevitable
God plays chess with what's left of our souls
but we're in control free will
and writing your secrets it will heal
that's why I write just for myself
I don't do this music to buy a nice house
so if no one listens
it doesn't really matter
cause' Dan's words were written
thus when my lyrics leave my flesh
my spirit's higher I live beyond death

there's other ways to attain this
make sure you're careful defining greatness
success isn't measured
except by the one whose death it is
double check that kid
process is the reward
if you don't got that then you got no hope
chasing women making a million
you really think that's gonna change what lives within
what if you never get a record deal
for real no label you still gonna create more fables
of those around you you found truth in my words

cause' when Sherv's in the vocal booth no it's not work
clouds and dirt gospel and church
can't climb mountain without a stepping stone first
walk across rocks on fire
to take your consciousness higher

when I improvise I improve my highs
but Cheeky's written lines seem to live in your mind
I studied fiction and philosophy
personal visions raps and beats
that's why this was meant to be
a different century
I'd be a poet in the streets
but this whole industry is misguided
most of what you see isn't even writing
I've been inspired since the start
trying to take you higher and live off my art
all I've got I'm not one for advice
when you say no freestyling or albums on Spotify
the thought in my mind
is that you is even more lost than I
yet you have attention right
but that's never what success meant to Dan
I guess I just aim way too high

Sometimes I Feel

This is for me 11 years ago
clearly depression eats at your soul
I know you in the hole and you can't escape
no faith full hate and the bullshit
who's the culprit who's to blame
maybe it's yourself look in the window pane
a reflection of 11 years ago
but the message extends to listeners yes you know
if you see me in you just understand
you can breathe through the blue
that suffocates your face
the deepest waters can choke your words
but you can be the one chosen
to have flow over your fears
it won't be easy
starts with responsibility accountability
and talking to your feelings deep
where your demons live
put your spirit at peace

slaying demons is the hardest thing about being
also the most rewarding so it's important
a war fought for yourself open the doors to hell
you'll find a portal to wellness
well this takes time
and no it won't break your mind
but you'll change your life
the strength isn't in resentment
in the depths of your spirit won't find revenge just
healing
here's the thing your imagination's ancient

it can put unconquerable monsters anywhere
they would know your worst fears
but you can disperse with the old house of mirrors
the illusion that everything is ruined
and you is just a human student
much learning is left on your path
I wrote this to Sherven mostly his past

getting out of a bad place
is way worse when you've got depression's sad face
old messages left on your phone
get left until who knows when
and old friends they keep calling you
but your soul's depths make you fall through the moon
lost in the galaxy
feeling there's frost on the fallen leaves
sometimes I feel this way
mostly since I turned 18
but doing what's meaningful to you
like music will heal your soul
so find what you need to grow
and the high road is often un-walked
it's easier to stop drop and fall
but stumble with the bolder of your goals
go full force towards God's throne

The Attic of the Pit

Lately I ain't been feeling hip-hop
it seems I want this dream for a quick love
for the attention when I'm wrecking onstage
but that's far away from God's page
I'm a reclusive author but I find music talks words so
I've got more
inspiration but sin awaits Dan
chasing famous for a basic bitch man
consider this a warning to myself
love's infinite but horny leads to hell
a bottomless pit where the problems grip
your ankles even Halos can't save you
escape through meaning and purpose killing Satan in
cursive
started rapping extending writing
loved freestyling but look what has been
I'm trapped within your acceptance
that's no way to make a track a hit or a pen live
I'm selfish right to the core
it's hellish but I just relish in this war

as the years goes on
I feel I ain't got the ears to listen to your songs no longer
and what really bothers me
is I feel like I've gotta keep outta public speech
so that's why my novels evolve more
if it's fictional no one spits on my soul
it's difficult enough to write shit
without your little quotes in my life kid
I don't know if it's the self-respect
or a fear of falling into hell's depths

but after seven years I'm ready
for an angel's tears to really shape me
a relationship not 18 misses
I'm sick of this living in abysmal pits
where I can't see light feel the divine or breathe without
writing
I need to feel alive again finding meaning inside of my
screaming
my expression about where hell is
a mix between Led Zeppelin and depression

don't check for Dan I'll be working
trying to find a purpose knowing I'm not perfect
I'm not worthless
when you make a purchase
of my merchandise I'd prefer that right
I've heard the mics since before her birth night
when little Sherv arrived alive
this verse it writes itself
far away from those pts of hell
where the devil finds work for idle hands
every idol I've had writes through death
fights for a new breath
not just for themselves
but for anyone who feels way less
if I can be half as great then I've made a name
I can take to the grave
and the aim has never been fame
but I could use some change
as they all say
I guess now it's played out
but just like this song it's heartfelt
I didn't really think I needed a chorus
because just writing I enjoyed it

I Try

Yo Nick I really miss you
I just wanted to rap about you not some sister
but more so I wanna talk torso to torso
so you're gone but your soul lives on
cause' the spirit realm is near to anyone
who can feel your heart
you said get your head out of books
I would but look I got a new cheque shit
and if you were here right now
to hear my freestyle or how I never fight with my child's
mother
you'd be like what the fuck dude
you must move on those opportunities human being
and the wisest man I ever knew
he never sat down to write his own tune
so you this one goes out to you whew

I got your logo on my wall
and your Logos you know it lives in my skull
man I'm even exercising meditating
my head's a great space again
except those intrusive thoughts
but that's just the nonsense of the darkest arts
people will think this is a nice story
little do they know I'm writing with you and the holy
so she wants to change Hailey's name
I write this on the page just for my friend
if you was here you'd say take the high road
wait you are here and I'm trying yo
I don't wanna get pulled down below
but that's how it feels when I open her notes

I'm just writing to live my life
let me tell you Nick I try

music makes me cry
because I use it to flew through the skies
who am I
I'm just a human being
trying to escape that cubicle I'll be in
and Nicholas always lives with us
don't ask a physicist ask those miracles
here we go I wanted to say thank you
cause' talking with the dead it can save you
I break through no angry texts
instead my pen sends my dead friend my response
and he hears me
you don't believe it
well what the fuck do you know about breathing lyrics
this mysterious is all around us
boundless like sound or love is
grudges I'm done with
keep it 100
no such thing as the setting sun keed

The Only Heaven There Is

The spirit exists clearly vivid
when I'm spitting lyrics shit kid since his
childhood I had a wild soul
but as I get older I find God's notes
I was never one for faith
in fact I felt that it was all fake
I was sitting with Class in his basement
and what he said stays in my head
he was talking bout his children
and how he makes sure they're believers
cause' you need to have someone to talk to
when what you're walking on falls through
made a point using his voice
bout his boys anointed they do more dope shit
interesting not as simple as it sounds but
yo he knows that so no bullshit
and the practical approach
of having a heavenly soul let's blessings unfold
messengers of old wrote it down so I just stole they
sound

there's a huge pit of darkness
it lives in my room in my closet
awful to look at filled with notebooks old crap
Rider Store paystubs separation papers
an affidavit from when I was insane shit
my cranium feels pain and alien
making sense of my fragmented past
at last Dan just wants to walk through the graveyard
but all these thoughts talking got me bogged down way

from the only heaven there is
finding meaning in the story you live
I was feeling low until that writer's soul found me a
better hope
yo you know that life is suffering
don't gotta go to Tibet with monks to learn it
nah kid you can stay in your days spent
without purpose or courage life is merciless
so create something great to place against your own pain

the real question is there a real heaven
afterlife when we pass into light
the atheist thinks it's craziness
but wait a minute we can't see the infinity
now Cheeky be looking at papers
that might change her last name
I don't wanna add gas to the flame
and I don't wanna appease like Neville Chamberlain
here's the main thing
suffering if I refrain and don't sign my name
I don't need to see another courtroom
unless I'm there as a journalist reporting
a fort moon to decide this
and I felt like I shouldn't sign it
but Nick said to take the high road
I'm gonna get the same result in the final
judgement so fuck it
I must live
done with stressing Sherv
it's probably better for her
so thank you Nick for living past the grave

What You've Done to Me

I've had heartbreak I've had betrayal
I've had dark days with nothing but Halo
I've made due stayed faithful to the angels
the only way they can save you
I heard once no rain no rainbows
I spit fire and flames volcano
the strange view which I do hold
is the worst parts of your past birth new hope
you've spoke a timeless sentiment
true gold finds you when you're dead inside
a better life awaits those who are responsible
for taming their own monsterful war
it seems impossible no
but heaven hopes
you overcome suffering for your soul

got some reasons to be resentful
they change with the season until he let go
somewhere between Camus and Van Gogh
you don't know either you don't know Daniel
hey yo I'm signing papers
so even in suffering remain so grateful
that'll change your
whole landscape sand and the lakes
and the man and his shape eh
it rains for days but the sun and it's rays
will soon emerge from the moon's Earth
too deep need to get to true speech
alright clarity of thought
that's what arrives when there's no arrogance in your
heart

easier said than done
when everything is running from the setting sun

classic material
an author with a lyricist's soul
but this braggadocio has gotta slow
kinda lost my point talking to noise
bitterness and sadness only live in his past life
if you asked me years ago
Dan'd think that must be a fucking miracle
but here we are nears the stars on the sphere of God
and what keeps me on this
revolving planet's
understanding
a better man lives
in the sonnets letters and books Dan creates
so what's your purpose
cause' the flood rushes
often unexpected
and if you wanna keep your head above the water
you're gonna need something with depths much deeper

My Morning

I wake up in the morning do what's important first thing
yeah you know Sherven meaning I check my phone
get myself outta bed then go down stairs
no cares allowed before the coffee drops
but first Sherv got a cig in his mouth
outside I'm about to die
cause' I gotta piss so I extinguish this cig then
I'm in the bathroom rap tunes from yesterday
get pressed and played in my head yes it is
an addiction an obsession with literature
if you take that shit away
it'd break my brain and then I'd be killing Sherv
yeah you feel these words
especially because you're listening to the same riddles in
my head
anyways I pour my coffee
usually warm from six in the morning
but that's too early for my non-existent girlfriend
now the clock swirls around 10 on the dot
I walk up to talk to my pops what

I drop on the couch my pops is a boss
so he's often talking with someone else
but that's cool cause' Dan's neural pool
could use a few molecules to solve a Rubik's Cube or
two
soon the coffee talks me online
got a match on Tinder who makes me sad and indifferent
the internet I ain't really into it
too many spider's webs trying to bite my neck
got an email chain from my publisher

.

89

it makes Cheeky's brain come online again
and my photographer got a new computer
well that's good cause' I need to see his new work
am I egotistical it's more that I can't sit still for a whole
hour
Bowser's advertised more so maybe I should play Zelda
well nah bruh this whole hour I'm smoking
re-pouring coffee filter soon I gotta get some real work
done
but first my pop is talking bout leaders
you gotta listen to your old people for real

yo Dad's got a Zoom meeting
so I put the music up in my ears then
go upstairs don't have enough jitters
that's okay I've just gotta get to business
first thing is this
make my bed awaken the LED strips
yeah I said it wrong but I'm still in your head kid
next I change outta jammies into exercise jammies
ride the stationary bike
often it's Classified or Drake and his rhymes
playing in my mind
then I'm feeling fine
eat a burrito I need a smoke too
before I got back to my room
the time has come for meditation session
next up I get washed up
listening to the best shit
Akira the Don making Jordan Peterson into songs
I'm feeling calm and in need of thought plus progress
so I sit my fat ass down
either gonna spit rhymes or the task at hand
is a novel
but y'all already know my soul

Free Fall

I'm a quiet dude when the silent mood
strikes me writing suffices
till my mind's spent then I'm just
aimless the days is bleeding together
in need of a lover
maybe Ayla would want to play more
down in Canmore and or Dan's Earth damn Sherv
so I send a message we was friends back then
always clicked in the old days we lived still
a lot has changed but I'm lost in her face
that beautiful music
human fulfillment
that's what I see but when I write to she
I don't know if it's right for me
I'm falling free

holy shit she actually responded
you know the kid Cheeky ain't used to be wanted
so I thought lots before I replied
like could this be God's love flowing through her mind
asked about her dog but I really don't care
damn and you got a new job well you have pretty hair
yeah I got hired to be the author
but I'd rather be up all night with you if we're being
honest
nah kid I kept it clean
cause' she could live in my dreams
yo I was busy at a photoshoot
it took a while before I got back to you
asked boo if she wanna grab a brew
Dan flew

sorry Dan I'm busy I'm not really in the city
oh right girl's rural and well her neural connections
are often softened by alcohol and less rest than
a person should get to function
so her rejection upended the pedestal I placed you upon
the devil's hold on your soul is strong
plus you're extroverted and I'm just a hermit
living at my parents' so why would we share a life
yeah you're funny but you love the country music
and no you're not stupid you just need some new friends
and to quit boozing and always dating losers
sorry you made my day
but I'm falling away

The Lost Woods

I ain't no genius do I look like Anthony Kiedis
I just keep on reading speaking listening to Peterson
so I think I need to go and clean my room again
nah you're overthinking
but now the soul flares within Dan
let me tell you a story
it's not about me myself well not only
archetypal meaning that the heart within you
sees reflections of scenes I paint here's the kid
lost in the forest talking to the nomads
but he wants to go home yo he don't got one
so instead his head is led by the steps of his friends
but then they all left him
now his quest he starts to resent
yet no repentance as he grows aggressive
without friendships now check it
his head is set on death fam

I ain't no liar and I ain't no messiah
at the end of the day I just say I'm a writer
insurmountable obstacles stop his soul
halted by the old deadwood of course
with his friends gone he musters on
with the skull of his thoughts enveloped in nots
doesn't have a loving friend
just wants someone to run with him again
but he's lost in the woods and talking to grudges
must have his love back but it won't happen
there's a mask on the ground
and now it's wrapped all around his skull
so he takes a vow to break every crown

all around him the fall sounds but no one calls him
so he marches on from dusk to dawn
to the very town where he was born
with a head full of horns
you've been warned

now he's a rolling stone in the roaring storm
that goes on at the throne he calls his home but yo
when he arrives he'd neglected
finds no respect and
all his best friends' depths are
making his mental health fall
but the worst part is his cursed thoughts
could be reversed fast
if he just reached out
but isolation puts mind in the basement
he finds an ancient tablet and grabs it
understands in his hands is magic
with his resentment setting in he lets go
of the pedestal of having a better soul
plays the devil's notes on the tablet
and pretty soon the city's moon crashes
it destroys his voice of redemption
and The Lost Woods' boy has no best friends
check the message

I Don't Wanna Be in Love

When I made this beat I wanted to say some shit
but the moment passed
a poet in raps
trying to show his chest and what goes in his head
a reminder to myself
I often wear Nick's shirt when writing in the house
it's got his logo and I got it from his mother last
December
and so Tinder was often a topic
subject of discussion but what's more interesting
is our convos about what love is
and if we would ever settle down with another lover
hmm
once you've gone through separation between parents
you is less inclined to find true love up in the form of
marriage
so I guess once you've seen the most heinous of
paintings
you start to wonder if you could ever become a saint
again

Dan's too honest set Hand'Solo Records
close the app reopen it yeah it's not good
Tinder addiction kills men now you feeling Dan
thought so yeah she hot but her soul
lacks the wholeness
oh shit just settle down
forever's in the now but so's the devil's crown
so this morning Jordan Peterson be keeping Cheek
strong
he even got Dan believing in God once upon a time

95

and I'm caught between wanting a queen
and being lost up in my dreams
cause' these songs scream parts of me loving myself
not putting another up on a higher shelf
why is this the case
I find I'm fine up in my space
all alone talking to notes that walked me through the
forest
back when no one wanted to know Dan

guess I'm focused and I feel love's an old friend
but I moved on to better things
let my letters be my queen
why am I thinking of a lover again
when the time is right I'll find my wife
right now my lifestyle can't get quite fowl
a devil in a bright violet dress
might be allowed up in my bed
but wow that would be a mistake
cause' cigarettes and sex are worth less
than a best friend
I'm eccentric independent academic schizophrenic
so I need a queen who makes my pen click
and yes that's a rarity
if she talks about Aquarius then I won't marry her
I guess intelligence is as important as her hard work
I stopped this search long ago
hoping Sherv's songs will find her soul

Find a Way

If I met myself what would I really think
you've got no wealth poor health but oh so much ink
drips
no tattoos afternoons are for rapping's muse
staring into space without a care on your face
pimples by the dimples of the schizo who lives at home
given a microphone by Jon Hill who liked his flow
but yo you should probably shower
let some water pour down on your fire but why though
you ain't hired your room is the office
you made your life good when Nick's tomb started
coffin
I was working in the public relations
imagine Sherven with budget pages
fuck that I said it
I'm a creative but I hate that label
you can't copy and paste my soul
like Paul Hill Business School

I guess I'm living my soul as an individual
and for the whole world I would want nothing less or
more
maybe you're meant to be a business person
but let's keep it real that's a pretty specific person
and your worth isn't in your bank account
I say to Sherven as I'm thinking out loud
now These Clouds Don't Quite Look Right
reminds eye of the dark parts of the book of my life
most people could write a whole memoir
but won't bleed their soul at night in the pen war

97

therefore they get up in the morning
and spent their cheques working on what's not important

the hardest part of life is to be yourself
the rest you can figure out with your business clout
I remember working at the office it's nonsense
it's a waste of God's gift
awfully honest almost to a fault
my conscience is too strong to try to do you wrong
but I'm far from perfect
and we all fall as the world spins
but your purpose will keep you deserving
of your own respect so you don't go to hell
is it a real place I don't know you've been there
and fate can deal hands that don't seem fair
but keep living your own life and you'll be okay
just need to find a way

What Do You Want From Me

Long live those songs who made you who you are
Eyedea was like Jesus Ali wrote the Quran
I used to print out raps Slug and Nas
and put those up on my brown apartment walls
my babymoms didn't seem poems
but it was images poems and stories I saw
who would have thought I'd be at Class' house
talking bout life and stuff and his art of rap
at the top of Canada's hip-hop
not for a wristwatch or just for big clout
but because his heart was really in it
could Cheeky from the prairie city be as infinite
I don't know but I hold this scroll
which goes out to those who got devout flows
who are wondering if they need this
yet making music keeps them breathing

what do I want from me a money tree
nah but that sounds like some funny sheit
some piece of mind when I leave this life
that's what Cheeky finds on the streets he drives
and when I write it's like I fight suffering
I give lucifer enough problems then
if the opposite begins and I get lost in the woods with
tigers than my words won't find truth
a non-writing writer is monster courting insanity
ask Franz Kafka b
oh you don't know him
well he wrote stories Metamorphosis

important thing is this
he found rewards in his work and purpose
even though the world didn't in his lifetime
he wasn't even recognized
if you can't get with that type a mind
you ain't no writer

I mean right now I'm reading bout custody
if I didn't have writing songs I'd be done for real
a record deal ain't gonna save you
put a meal on your table
but I need fables to be here
novels help too
even the autobiographical of Luke Boyd whew
yeah I'm cool when I want to be
but that's not often I just talk on beats
doesn't even matter if people listen
of course it boosts the ego of rapper Sherven
the process' progress is all we have fam
if you don't got that you don't got rap
success is being yourself
and somehow cashing cheques
into your bank account
that's what I want from me
so yo what's up keed

FIVE

Image in Writing

Soul on Fire

Which path do you want to choose
whichever wolf you don't feed will lose
who's to say the muse is her face
when her soul is fire the goal of desire
higher than lust a writer I trust it's love
often unspoken lost in emotion
the frost on her doorframe is the cost of opening
but is it wrong to want what's hot
negative connotation begs to live as a woman
and for Dan there's no poem without her source of love
could there be more to us
than a momentary point of touch
not sensual but intellectual
it begs the question no
could you let me into your own soul
forget the depths of despair
and set your heart on our prayer
where you're the heir to my air

you're a positive light in my bottomless night
and if I can climb from the depths of dying
to clutch what I am then maybe love is in a friend
but I don't expect my pen to correct what's less
unless what I said repents lust in my head
sex is meaningless
without respect for the chest of the evening's kiss
that spark of divinity in the heart you're giving me
otherwise a lover's thighs plummet your demise
running from her eyes which summon light
because your soul's on fire
I feel it's burning when you speak in sermons

and the reason I need yours
is because it's meaningful
if you'd hold my poetic soul
we'd grow old without broken bones
the whole world would need to know
you chose my words
but not my form

the spiritual goal is no more miserable soul
so if you didn't show what lives in your skull
I wouldn't have given you my notes
I don't know why we trust each other
maybe when we die and can watch forever
we'll see how time's watch wound us together
passing years never asking for ears
then unmasking fears and shattering appearances
it's as clear as this time piece my mind thinks
but you're Daoist and I'm more Socrates
you're lost in the East and I'm at the crossroads street
but talk is cheap
unless it unlocks what's deep
there's frost on our feet so we need some hot heat
but not like animals more like Michelangelos
there's fire in your soul and I would know
cause' Daniel burns

Leaves

Do I love you or want your trouble
I'm wondering if it's the same thing those phrases
your face is amazing and you're insecure about it
you're astounding
surround Dan with your boundless
crown of lust
a thorn from roses that scourges emotions
[redacted]
[redacted]
your oceanic consciousness
is more than Dan's allowed to live
I would put a crown on your head
just to drown in your mess
and be found in your loss
is it awesome you make spirits possess me
when you're talking it's lyrics your breath leaves
was us written in the stars or given by God
a random encounter planned by the Prime Mover

self-discovery in someone else loving me
hell isn't fallen leaves but your autumn springs
a waterfall of all her thoughts The Author scrawls
not me the God King
I don't want you to leave
I've got to explore your soul's core
and bare your bare fears you're therapy
just share the air I breathe
you're crazy like me scrawling phrases that speak
and your ways are deep like the cosmos
God knows I want your soul
and when you confessed about the dress

105

in your head and what it meant
when the day's rain was wet
my chains weren't set
angels fly free and I'm grateful our minds speak
before the day morphs and time leaves
the hourglass so how long will ours last

a man can't put a chain on an angel
and Dan would feel lame trying to contain you
you're a galaxy and all you ask of me
is to have a seat at your table
with sadness and grief angel
even when you're leaving
I'll still find Eden meaningful
it's too much to want true love with your heart
and expect you to stay put
when death awaits your brain and thoughts
could it still work it's possible
only God would know
but I won't force your home
I guess I wrote those notes
to point out what I go through
wanting to hold the moon
before the stroke of noon
did I do this justice I must have
because what's in my head just
got less heavy
when the levee breaks
a wedding ring doesn't mean anything
guaranteed

Album or Novel

I can't tell if you're an album or a novel
listening on repeat but wanna read to the cover
you bleed from love's words
more agreeable than numb Sherv
and I need to know your heart's source
your thoughts purge the darkest curse
of those Lost Woods forests
the source of us is two souls who touch
I won't rush to hug the lushness of yourself
and our house if you're sworn as spouse
of course holds much
two doors is more than enough
one room's about the music you put out
or the muses you've found
and the blueprints allowed
for my own vault that portal is locked
where Dan's own core must talk
until lover's stare into space
unearthing the very faces you and I created

album's repetition's always welcomed within the man
and allowed to begin at the end where vowels syllables
blend
but wow this is simplistic the language of English
can transcend this schizo's brain
to give you a page of my narrative
that won't hit the aim of sharing a life
my arrogance fights while your marriage is with a mic
but you carry it's strife for the burial of your night
and your airless height makes me embarrassed to reply
you heritage finds carriages in the sky

107

where your American patriot and Arabic terrorist cry
why
historically this war in she is more to me
about where me my mind and I've been
colliding with your kaleidoscope
wondering if I lie to my soul
but overthinking's no novel or album
so I'm out son

maybe you're a conceptual album
or a philosophical fiction that I need to grow more
wisdom
not in you or that's probable
but in my dome and the bars you wrote
I'm lost in your oceans
anchored on your shore's coastlines
I spoke my mind and your soul replies
you told me what I am
and noted the coal's fires
two hopeless writers
united unbroken undivided I must find it
shining like a lighthouse
in rhyme meter and your white blouse
I won't fight with your cause
to right your past I'll triumph the dark
by igniting what's wrong
it's all my fault
I don't trust
but that word is the source of love
and I can overcome the soldier's gun
pointing at everyone
through heaven's drums
and writing you songs
that sound like heaven's thoughts

Disappoint

that's what I told her a bold move
while she's laying in her bed nude
a sad dude woke up
broken love cause' she's floating above
I get squashed shit God
am I supposed to live a bachelor
an averager rapper without no damn muse
this afternoon the saddest tunes from the blackest blues
cause' she has to move
chasing dreams amazing screams
a replacement for feelings still want to taste your
demons
six months 'til his lust is leaving
it sucks but this lust needs Jesus
if we run to Eden then I'll fall in season
but I'll hold your grief's end
believing Sherven's poison
is the evening of this woman
doing what I shouldn't

[redacted]
[redacted]
I've said your strength your wet with sweat
but already left on a jet intent for the best
a sad day that'll pass away I ask me
if she's a flask of gin or a passion
and when Dan's cig flickers out
a bitter mouth this sister left
she's given much driven because
she's feeling herself as a spirit ought to
it's not flashing her assets to Dan

that grabs what I am
it's the very drags of her flame
and the begging of her legs
that saves me from the end
so do you dance while the music's playing
or get sad cause' it's losing the feeling
the woman doing what she shouldn't

oh ye of little faith your story's only a page
saved by amazing grace that escapes into taste
the carnal desire of animals' dying words
but the Cardinals I know wouldn't start a fire
just to find warmth
a leap of faith to a demon's cave
could kill Dan's days
or even build upon his base instincts
if she's history before her soul gets to me
then infinite breathes right in its leaves
the temptation of the desert
is death awaiting without repentance
she's forever but you're not
the door locked
but Dan's got a battering ram
and it's called the thoughts in his head
I won't force it
if the door swings
then there's more of she
but this woman

Louvset

I'm exhausted and I'm talking nonsense
all these problems from one woman
I haven't showered why would I
it's a waste of my time
when your face is mine but you change what I am
I was looking for a matrimony
and this woman only wants me to stab her holy
and you know me I'm boring
and the old friend who's soul I met
when the world was so dead
just wants to be a girl in my bed
but she's way too hot she slays my thoughts
while raising gods I praise no longer
songs were my self-expression
'til this sister licked your heart's neglecting
an invention of wishful thinking
this old schizo and the little woman's kiss slowed
but wait one minute the spirit is still connected
[redacted]

ask Ali my brother
it's not so much that I won't love you
it's more so that I won't trust you no closure
when you close your door and move your home
I'll be all alone talking to those love poems
you're a substance I must have
but love's sad when touch is had and no cost is bought
a transaction of Dan and a woman's head
when Brooklyn's meant as your book and destiny
honestly a girlfriend's constant working
when God gift's these poems with your Being woven

111

deep within them
and a friend with benefits is this planet's stench woman
Dan loves your handcuffs
but that sentence sums up
the blessing for which I seem to quest
yes

our intelligence matches my conscientiousness surpasses
asking if opposites attract when
love and lust clash in bed
handcuffs on your wrist
sound like I'm losing my death
but improvement begins with importance first
so woman are you cursed
or the gift this kid needs
just to really live big
whence your head rests against my chest or neck
is my life more fulfilled
or in a war of the lore's religions
my battery's low and I'm asking for your soul
when Commandments of old
aren't understanding those hopes you hold
to morph into the form of my words until
the morning's mourning
where we separate like amoeba
then come again because Eyedeas
and our feelings are freed then

Afterdark

I'm an artist it just means I'm honest
it's dangerous but yes I aim for love
the problem is I'm falling off a cliff
my stomach hurts I can't eat
I have to sleep but yo Dan's dreams
with caffeine will ask for that fiend
[redacted] as love hits her and lust lives more
insanely beautiful like a painting by Michelangelo
the angels know I'm trying to find me
and walk God's path
but the thought of she has
me willing to live a bit and twist her spirit
'till [redacted] must win and substance
touches just us trusting but why
when goodbye must fly
across the continent of lost in your dreams

I'm barely functioning
your airplane's a gust of wind
take you the angel to a plane full of what your face holds
a spatial dimension where hate in your soul
fluctuates away to nil
and now your smile has a devilish twinge
which suffocates sin
and I must say it with a pen
but heaven upends all mortal aims
when a temporal game is played
to win what a soul doesn't own to live
and the worst part of my bursting heart
is the thirst for your darts could work out
in the months or collapse into nothing

113

then it's substance wasn't and it's just
shush Dan
I'll censor my pencil's tip
no more devil's grip

we only work cause' love's the source
and once the dirt is the focus
we'll be broken
choking on ashes of just what's happened
it saddens me to napping
ideally feeling she cuddling
but that discussion's in the future
after I move you
and force your muse to a publisher
then run to my words and love your courage
but despise your eyes shining at goodbye
so should I
it would be fun said your tongue
and I want it
but would it be the best
eloquence we express
ties our minds into a final state
where vinyl decorates our heads and space
so it could work out
and your mouth isn't Medusa
I don't want my music blue
so I say no to lucifer

Outside

Writer's block even though her lighter's hot
feelings gone no I need her more than ever
we were talking for two hours
thoughts of her inner child
how her father being a worker
disturbed the
balance of the palace
where her stanza's sad hurt was dormant
I ain't morphine I want her morphing
approaching not ferocious but open
to show him emotional content
vulnerable her loving soul
and the trouble that glows when
he's overwhelmed at home
and controlling the outcome
rather than solving the problem
before it blossoms into nonsense
rocks the household
with an outburst of lost guilt
it's just hurt souls

easy for me to believe on the outside
of the house on fire where your blouse gets whiter
I hope I don't sound pious bias when I suggest
your mind's vault will solve the crimes against
if you show your soul and know the goal isn't anger
and your emotional maturity
will force a note that burns the speech
hurts the people in a miniscule sense
a miserable defense is possible
but your father's whole Being

wants to hold the secrets you're keeping deep down
and the inner child's simple desire
to live more aligned with
the parents who shared a life
and raised you as right as the day before the night
they'll stay while you cry
to make the rain fire
Outside

you don't ask about it
so I rap my thoughts out
the shroud just won't cut it
the cloth is too see-through
your review
of deep moods
from little you
scribbled a new tune
and I just picked up the tool
and let the spirit emerge into
the physical manifestation
you're listening to
as I rap my face off
confrontation
isn't what I want you to take on
I'm just saying
if you lay down
your brain's thoughts
you'll be amazed at
what a statement creates
it's love
otherwise
the heart in your mind
wasn't communicated
and you'll lose the pain's chance
to tool it

116

into great trust
so say what's sacred
and change the way the rain's felt
what

Memento Mori

Authentic never meant shit in the set I live
the death of his music looms when
a book cheque does arrive
should I focus on poems
or morph into words more simple
less meaningful the quest to bleed my soul
for you to read alone the deepest quotes
are in the screaming notes of reason and chords
I need that to be whole
but the world approves more
of novels I wrote for who
you said the globe needs my music
in the moment I was weak and useless
you speak the true shit deep like the movement
of losing yourself in a beautiful groovy bounce
where loose lips shout about
what's in the head heart and thought
honestly the problem he feels
is I'll be abandoned by people
while onstage unlike on the page
but the song remains of the darkness you saved
when you started barking your heart's phrase

I hear it the lyrics even when I'm sleeping
another dream again about me freestyling
keeps me alive while dead
I try to read but find my steps take me away
from phrases on the page
I'm raised from death when I play the sentences of
aggressiveness
and I'm blessed with this

gift of language which lifts his sadness
and all that Dan has carried too long
I'm married to thoughts but rarely the jotted version
it's the songs words that I start in the morning
but the poison of introversion keeps me wondering
if thunder and applause isn't living in the wondrous
God's
summer of plans for the rapper Dan
but you answer with your response
Memento Mori

people respond when I freestyle my heart
but to bleed for this art
I need to leave the plot of land
where I stand and command a crowd of hands
when I want peace quiet deep and silent
but your greenlight is rhyming
telling me a bestselling album could happen
nah fam
I'm imagining that outcome
is that what I want though I don't know
old souls
told gold Memento Mori
remember your story mortal
don't forget your going to die
so float to the sky
before your death arrives
then no regret arrives
and when I'm dead I want to be a writer
but also a rhymer
and that's why I find your words
playing inside my own skull

Lost

I hate this beat it plays in my ears
and creates fear I won't be enough
I'm bored with talk I want more of your heart
but you're busy when I'm in the city
miserable my scribbled soul
is indifferent to words about capitalism
from a mouth that's trapped in the distance
psilocybin isn't alive when
a soldier's aim is your sober brain
mircodosing's no psychosocial rehabilitation
only rehab of what's left within the woman
we'll lift the curses in your past
trapped by what's happened I started rapping
cause' I can't respond to sad thoughts I had a lifetime
ago
but writing rhymes in flow

make sin's aim miss the mark
let me kiss your heart
drifting apart is what this feels like
cause' you need a steel pipe just to be alright
I did that lived it infinite
it wasn't until I was done with drugs
that what I was it fell away
hell's rain awaits your self's plane
if you don't stop the war of your chorus
and my [redacted] is just boring
cause' you're in a mental trap
where the devil laughs at your body hottie
yes it's kicking just like karate
and honestly you texted me

as I'm writing
but hell's pit isn't enlightenment
so I don't want to check the light on
my phone
to see why you're grown and I'm wrong

you're not mature enough and it hurts my cause
cause' I'm searching for stars working for love
I don't deserve it
because what you want is just to float about
through oceans and dirt good luck with that
all you lust after is a good shush
I need some space to be alive again
and find the aim of the wanderer
lost at bay
and what do I want from me
just thoughts and feelings
but your body I need it
it's just too bad that
I'm busy loving your spirit

SIX

Music Saves the Soul

Just Like the Rain

It's almost impossible to explain
but I owe almost all I've wrote to the rain
and I'm so sick of this suffering
makes the kid wanna go download Bumble again
wandering in search of the woman
wondering if Sherv's meant to have a person
or if his purpose is a world which
doesn't extend beyond his own head
nah that's no entendre
wandering in the tundra
must have something for Dan
hoping in the act of writing
it shows him that in rap there's a light switch

transcendent
if Dan said it Dan meant it
when the rain pours
make your brain soar
nah not the harmful
I'm talking bout thoughts from Aristotle
that you and I could walk to
the whole reason I've got your ear pressed
is because I know the feeling
when the eve's wet
those rain drops
always stain lots
but raise up your thoughts
away from what's wrong
paint some art
or even play my song
a way to capture the catastrophe

that's part and parcel of our lot in Being
if you got that feeling
then you can go ahead and leave the rain

I just like the rain
we must have it in Being
dress rehearsal
for what's gonna hurt you
plus it makes the curtain move too
when it starts pouring
you see whose heart is horrid
who thinks that they're the most important
all the thoughts dormant rush out
no journaling cause' they in a hurry again
the sky is falling
while they mind stalls and
I'm just jotting down all the problems
that's how I transcend Dan's head
where it's always raining
even on these pages
but that's the way that
the painful just
seems to create us

Cry Sis

When there's a crisis I wanna be like Mike was
beautifully giving a eulogy with a wrist watch
Nick's gone but his soul lives on
especially when Michael K gives his thoughts
I sing a song for a king and the crown
which screamed and drowned
while hit by a truck in the middle of the dark
there isn't a God
that's some thinking which won't solve
the miserable instances of existence we haven't
grabbed at tragic 'til it happens
that's when sadness traps us masks love
until someone stands up then what
I was sitting at the celebration of light
children of the light pilgrims in the night
listening to Mike with Nick's wristwatch
which died around 3:45
the time when the truck made him fly
and heaven and hell they did collide
the question left to ask yourself is why

Nick's father I was never close to
but showed so much composure without closure
that I know you're
the bolder the broken family's divorce wounds moved
on
you're strong in the face of tragedy
like a stone your face wasn't shattering
stoic in emotions that would force most of us into no
more love
that example was to Daniel

the way of handling life's unravelling
Ramble On said Led Zeppelin
death and strength in one person
I've been overthinking this album after all that's
happened
I can't imagine how to capture in rap words that hurt
tell the story was Nick's advice
well I'm in a hurry just to write
because life is gone in an instant
but infinite and transcendent

Jackie's happiness fell off a cliff
after a part of herself no longer lives
the death of her son sets the sun on everything
and here I stand with tears in my head and an ear to lend
it's all I've got in the fall to dark
I play a small part in the love of God
if Nick was living he'd be making buildings named after
Sherven
if I was the person who's curtains were closed and
it's the least I can do to speak to you
if you need to move to your son and the truth
play this tune and know he's with you
I know I do
when the falling moon and the suffering swoon
into doom and gloom
but it's only a matter of soon
before we meet him again in the heavenly realm whew

The Logos

One time I went out to the bar
and a dumb man asked me where I are
said he saw my car at the university
he was wondering what became of my learned degrees
not much but I trust God
I didn't really respond to his miserable thoughts
he thought life is just a checklist
it's too bad you're defenseless and resentful
while my pencil has the essence of soul
and you're desperate just to find a better home
I'm schizophrenic it took a little while
plus I'm a single parent who has a little child
university it took me longer
but I don't really hear where the fuck your songs are
published novelist at 27
I'm authoring my own life don't be jealous of a legend

people will doubt your creative work
until they're holding the pages of your book
they'll talk a lot about how you're not a rhymer
until they hear it your lyricism then it's silence
keep trying it's not important
what these dying men think deserves more respect
it's your life so grab the gold mic
be as bold as the knight who foretold what shines
I've been on this path for so long
that I really can't hear the laughing of the lost
it's not easy to do
and that's why I jot for Cheeky
and well definitely not you
that's not hostile that's just rock and roll

Aristotle taught more
than an asshole at a bar cares to learn
so you can throw your shade at Sherv
but I'll still glow like those rays of gold

I came from the days of old
to make my name known
thoughts are a long-term investment
that's why it took a little while
for the songs of Sherv to get pressed and played
but yo I'm just afraid of being average
being an asshole to a passing stranger at the bar like no
I'm not really interested
schizophrenic's investments in a better self pay more
dividends than
an engineering businessman's simple head can
I'm meaning meaning not mean and mean ends
and my cash flow is trash and slow
but yo at least I'm not the asshole and resentful
cause' the passion in my soul
is just ashes in the snow
these Logos raps are cold
so you have to know
when it's time for I to die
the one thing you can't say is he didn't try to write
so find your own life
it's free you can pay me no mind

Free

People think I'm wound too tight
but I just feel I've found true light
freedom equals discipline
believing Sherven's sick with a pen
Auschwitz had a sign which said
work will set you free it hurts my head
to see irony about a killing spree
but here's the thing of what it means to me
the only time I feel positive
is when I'm writing with all my gifts
Auschwitz is atrocity
but responsible me found some peace
I need a burden to carry
otherwise Sherven might as well be buried
where he finds the most meaning
is living in accordance with my spirit
clearly

there's no freedom in being a demon
keeping secrets instead of living
if you speak the truth to people
you'll be amazed at the boulders that move you
being responsible is difficult
but you'll slit you throat
if you live in a void
carry a cross and make it heavy
whether you believe in God or Led Zeppelin
this religious ideal
lives in us regardless of what you believe so
if you want to conquer the monsters
who live in your closet then be responsible

it's the only option you have
to stop the constant problems of man
and this story's older than you are
about as old as a quasar that takes stars

life is suffering you can understand that
even if you're dumb as shit
the counter balance to our sadness
and tragic is just to act right
I'm not a prophet
I don't even got a profit
I'm just talking the obvious common sense
you're walking on this path
and all of a sudden you're attacked from the dark
what's the solution to the problem
to lay out your blueprints way before you're falling
in other words to be responsible
so you're strong and good
before you walk in the woods
then you have a chance
to deal with all the trash
that's part and parcel
of walking in a dark world
so it's on you
to be responsible
and free your soul

Homer Simpson

The meaning of life
a baby screaming in the night
from zero to four nah I didn't snore
but five to nine man the time flies
soon my child will be zooming and driving
right now the light dial is shining brightly
while I'm writing I've been responsible
but that hardly compares to a parent's soul
down with the patriarchy
made me not allowed to care for my daughter jeez
this is a bit much alright let's give it up
life's tough but I'm so privileged
that I don't have the privilege of living with my kid
you add the schizophrenic diagnosis
and get the fuck outta here with your oppressive bullshit
oh I know you're so oppressed
and that's why you can't even make your bed

here's the thing
this suffering oppression's real
but you gotta learn how to deal
earn a meal in spite of it all
cause' we can't discern who has the worst fall
all involved have odds against them
and all involved have God as a best friend
but the message about oppression
is if you have direction and you're a white man
you don't deserve the life you spend
in fact it's in writing in human resources
in every student's notebook and homework oh shit
did you ever notice this collective bullshit

approaches whiteness as hopeless
worse than that as racist
and now the phrase white supremacy
doesn't even mean white supremacy
I don't have to rhyme you feeling me

are people racist
yeah you dumb basic bitch
but the solution isn't demonizing humans
to consider whiteness life ending
is the same thing which you claim you're fighting
against
that's racist
and I don't wanna make this song
it just came out of my brain's thoughts
I'm indifferent
I don't give a shit what your race is
I just wanna know if you can melt faces
with phrases
but I felt I had to say this
just to stop some hatred you stupid ass racist
I can't be complacent placing historical guilt
on a bunch of little kids
I know you flipping all this privilege
but you should think a bit in the mirror
racist

Stumble Uphill

This morning I feel worthless
it's not surprising when you look at last night
stayed up way too late
trying to make love on a dating app
my brain's washed from chasing lust
but that's the way the game devolves
when you wake up and the day starts
you pay the cost for your mistakes at dusk
suffering you caused
fucks with your head
more than new scars that cut
and the only wat to evolve
is slowly moving up to God
I'm not following the concept
your life will be hollow
without clouds of what's next
right now I don't wanna write no
I'd rather wallow in sorrow
without a tomorrow

forward requires more words and writing
to fight with last night's death of what I am
trying to climb up to light's path
and see if I can ignite what's left
it seems very difficult
but I'd be feeling more miserable
if I didn't wrote
I'd rather shower and play Halo
but now your powers would lay low stay focused
I know it's hopeless but the only chosen path
is to go in against the dark

and hope what Dan spoke
will allow an old note to somehow float above
opening my problems and soaking in wrong paths
might shine a light on a bright tomorrow
at least that's what I'm hoping
feeling broken and in need of a poem oh man

as I stumble uphill I must will
this lust to be killed and feel love without guilt
difficult to say the least
spilling ink feeling he's healed
freedom is responsibility
that's why Jesus scarred his knees
on the hills of Galilee
stumbling up to death
carrying a burden and buried for the world's sin
and Sherven can't even put words down
too busy working on the next girl then
hurting when the curtain gets pulled down
so should Dan find a new source of fun
I think so cause' the morning is cursed at dawn
when I don't stumble up to the City of God
miserable thoughts got you feeling like killing yourself
I think you're in need of love

The Meaning of Music

Hailey has a recital for piano
and Daniel the asshole doesn't wanna go
it's not so much because of her
but her mother
and all the hurtful burning notes
words don't capture my sadness anguish
and pain that my past has
but transcendence
if Dan just picks his pen up
and goes through a sentence of what is left
in essence there's no replacement for this father
because he never abandoned his only daughter
and if the other family doesn't like it
oh well that's fine I'm busy writing
I'm just tryna say I love Hailey
so I put up with the rain and Nick said
to handle it with class
but shit fam Daniel is an ass
I'm giving what I can
even if it means listening to the past

I guess I just don't wanna check-in
with people who make me feel the opposite of heaven
lost in a sentence that lasts a lifetime
at least writing gets these feeling out
so I don't feel the need to scream with my mouth
but really it's not about me
my best decisions come from rerouting my selfish
that's what happens when you having children
build them instead of destroy yourself
feelings that bring joy to your house

what a relief when having a kid
there's no more need to only think about me
and I guess right there is the path right
I don't have to relight the past fires
that night died more when I decided
to listen to the recital
of my child's soul

Daniel doesn't wanna go
but the fact is music saves the soul
the beautiful human expression
even if you've been ruined by your own selfish
well this is a fact of life
it's part of the reason why I grab the mic
a small sacrifice is made
so Dan faces stepdad and the wife eh
it's not a big deal I'm living with God
spitting what's real so even in the valley of death
there's no shadows who can deal me hell
there's no enemies left in me
so I can be friendly listening to melodies
don't matter to me whatever the key be
I just need to be seen by Hailey
while she's playing
music to save the soul

Creation

The unknown's been calling me
it's either love poems or God in Being
I capitalize that last word I write
because it's what God's covenant is founded upon
built like a cathedral
to eliminate the guilt we all feel and evil
that's a problem hard to solve but
freedom in Being is why greed lives see fam
if we couldn't make the wrong choice
we wouldn't have names songs or a voice
we'd be automatons and all of our thoughts
would be predestined but see they isn't instead
we have free will so Being be real
we need to be people who feel evil
otherwise The Author's writing is nonsense
but we're most alive when all of us walk God's path

seems impossible to dream of God as love
when most people feel that he's not with us
and most of my friends are atheists
you can embrace that
I ain't dumb I used to
but the beautiful and transcendent
like the musical notes and death's grin
beg the question
if the life we're living is all there is
I find fault in that sense
because life is too strange
to not be scribed by a sage
the joyful sorrow of your new tomorrow
commands your moral imperatives

139

even if you only see spiritual in your therapist
and you know being a parent spoke of
something up with the forest
where the heir is home

that place where you escape to with a great tune
isn't that different from the infinite true
and the nature of religious experience
creates a movement to the significance
of living as us
if as a lyricist I can point you there
then God's gift scribbled this
and my voice is just air
that's the placement all the phrases aim at in creation
making sense of the angel's flight
day and night
the eternal recurrence
of the journal in my world is
the surest bet
to be heard by the light
it's a simple process
for the schizo God is love
but can be tough as a father ought to
yet at the end of the day
I just pray
that the music saves the soul

The Narrative and The Objective

People are so dismissive of religious
miserable souls think political suffices
a substructure to love each other
but without a God that's up above us
their doctrines are more stringent
than anything given by religious
the myth is there's utopia
but there isn't there's only broken souls
virtue signal all your wokeness
if you don't will hurt you and all your goals kid
transcendent's our ideal
that man's mission is just to rebuild
an imagined naïve assumption
that's capitalism is what's wrong when
not everyone's a neurosurgeon
and communism won't solve the problem

let me tell you about insanity
and when Dan saw a manic rabbit run at me
essentially the schizophrenic disease
places meaning where there isn't any
everything becomes significant
and it makes your brain just deteriorate
it's a religious feeling
but of heaven and hell both being beneath man
the political is very similar
when an ideologue doesn't believe in God
we have a religious impulse
and the political doesn't fit the bill

141

it's an attempt to set God and the moral ideals
in the political sphere of us
but rather than a culture
developed over centuries
it's whatever the hell will help them win

back to the schizophrenia
it attacks your brain and gives you plenty of meaning
but it's misguided your neurons misfiring
put you on as a higher man
inspired even if you're dying
but what's interesting
is the sense of meaning your senses feed your brain
the narrative you're telling yourself
can be embarrassingly wrong leads to pits of hell
but while you're imagining what's happening
the real world and what you feel in your soul touch
so what the fuck is up
you notice it even when your brain's healthy
not overloading with dopamine
people think it's a religious feeling
it makes the myth you're living real
I just hope we can all be healed

A Little More Heaven

So my daughter has a new stepsister
but honestly that's not really of interest to Sherv
I once knew a prisoner
Nicholas Dinardo and this is where my thoughts go
he has bipolar and is schizo
once he phoned this dunce who lives at home
from the prison telephone
the official let me know
well actually he asked me yo
are you Dinardo's lawyer
nah bro I'm just a journo
oh well do you wanna talk to him
yeah dude put him through to my line
next hear the prisoner talk more about hell's road
in a jail home where his self wasn't alone
because the shadow would attack his soul
in segregation death awaits him

he's had suicide attempts
I'd have to go back to my loose leaf to check
how many times he's almost died
he eats razor blades and needs to have his case
taken seriously
but I'm just making lyrics breathe
and his brain's disease
creates these hallucinations true statement
shadow awaits him a creation of Satan
said that only saying Jesus would save him Amen
I ain't playing his day's spent
writing help on his prison wall in his own blood
shoved by the guards

and forced to be put on a restraining board
good lord
the power of writing is to shine words
on the darkest parts of our own world

I've been trying to tell his story
through my writing and sell it for me
it's far from boring and there's more to this
but journalists they stay away from me
maybe that's wise I don't wanna be televised
for the hells I write but his jailed nights
seem to me worth publicity
music saves the people so you need to know
he's a human being losing feeling
in the dungeon of a prison
and no one wants to listen
still fam I feel a responsibility
cause' what he wants from me
is not just trust in his story
but more so a vehicle
to a new tomorrow
where he doesn't cut holes in his body
to stop the shadow
from attacking his own soul
and now you know

144

A Little More Heaven – Hidden Freestyle (Improvised)

One time I was at a rap battle
and this young Indigenous kid comes up to me and he
says
you don't even battle these guys
you profess
smart kid

Here we go the parables they rock my soul
because I talk to ghosts and then I'm lost in notes
I'm obnoxious indulgent I might say fuck it
the subject of every discussion
it's discussion I must win
oh damn I misspoke
doesn't matter rapper either way you get his joke
you is wishing you could kick it the way I do
I'ma slay you and your crew so you make room
pray to the moon before it squashes
everything you're talking cause' I'm lost within
my consciousness the audience is
expanding like a rubber band
cause' I command the land where I stand and
I'm the dopest to ever live
so I spoke this treasure and it was just so big
like Biggie is
welcome to the city kid
where Cheeky smokes a ciggie then he gets lit
understand me I'm breaking through the boundaries

of everything that's known as sound and speech
plus the poetics yes I go get it
like The Black Keys
Attack and Release cause' that's Cheek
now as the beat starts to collapse
I see the evening inside of the trap
of my own mind state the crime rate the blind faith
don't no no no no divine hate
shining the greatness you can try to copy and paste this
but you Kant like Immanuel

that's how I rap a flow
and every plateau I smash through
and you have to move
because the passion that's in my own soul
is so divine that I see my mind as goal
I'm just climbing higher
redefining fire and it burns me
you heard Cheek yes I deserve peace
chilling back feeling raps yes I'm a villain that's
coming for you cause' I'm running to the moon
like Majora's Mask I be holding the soldier's flask
broken that's
what happens in the past
I escape it
greatness
music saves the soul

Printed in Poland
by Amazon Fulfillment
Poland Sp. z o.o., Wrocław

87372241R00090